"We have had Fred Sarkari into our organization numerous times to speak and train our people and he has always walked away impacting their lives, Fred thank you for making a difference in our organization.

Fred Sarkari has an important message for us all. This book is a reflection of principles that every individual should be aware of, it is a must read. A powerful book that will help you be a more effective leader by igniting passion and purpose into your life and the lives of others.

All my employees and customers will receive a copy from me."
**Michael Butler, President, Northwest & Ethical Investments**

"Fred's 7 Principles of Great Leaders took me from university grad to author and a six figure income in less than 24 months! These principles are essential and timeless. This book is a must read!'
**Nolan Matthias, Author of *Golf Balls Don't Float***

"You have really assisted me in working towards achieving my vision, goals and dreams" at work, but more importantly in life. You're very inspirational!"
**Andrea Barton, Manager, Customer Service & Sales, Wells Fargo Financial Retail Services**

"I learnt so much from your course and it really has changed my life for the better. I am much happier both at work and at home because I am now motivated to be the leader in my family (to make an impact on my children and wife to form a great team and raise our children to be self sufficient). I like for you to know as a leader in your industry, you have made a great impact in my thinking. "
**Paul Cardwell, BMW**

"I am happy to tell you that your session was, by far one of the most impactful in recent memory. I was impressed with your speaking abilities"
**Patrick Nelson, Director, Public Affairs and Communications, Ontario Medical Association**

"Thank you for sharing your wealth of knowledge and experience. I finished reading your book and what an inspiring book!!!! Learned a lot and I have committed myself for 15 minutes daily on how I can be a better leader than yesterday."
**Raul Zapanta, IT Manager, Sleep Country Canada**

"Fred's great skill is to bring the 7 principles of great leaders vividly alive through the use of real life anecdotes. Add to that his relaxed natural grace and charm in presenting the principles, leaves you with an uplifting and inspirational must-read book."
**Mark J Hollingsworth, Director of Development Renfrew Educational Services**

"A very enjoyable read and thought provoking. Apply some of Fred's principles, they will make you better at what you do and who you are."
**Al Nasturzio, Vice President, Nexient Learning**

"I wanted to thank you for the information provided in your book. Your information on Commitment has helped me regain my focus and direction in my business by recognizing and changing my own behaviour.
I feel inspired and enthusiastic, and I am passionate once again about my work. Thank you for reigniting my passion and purpose."
**Andrea Thatcher, President, Body Sense Wellness**

"Fred's 7 Principles are derived from Fred's "real-life" experience. The 7 disciplines are truths we must acknowledge to achieve what we set out to do in our respective lives"
**Jonathan Weaver, President, Peak Performers**

"I read your book and found the message truly words to live by. An inspiring and motivating read."
**Joe Santos, MCAP, Regional VP and Mortgage Brokers Association of British Columbia President**

"Fred, your commitment to making myself accountable in this game of life has given me a sense of clarity and an action plan in pursuing my purpose with passion and direction. You helped me get out of doing the same things in life, just for the sake of doing them. Thank you for giving me the opportunity to live my life with passion, and the courage to follow my purpose."
**Ryan Miles, West Jet**

"I read your book the same night I received it. I found the book to be enlightening and I just couldn't put it down until I finished it at 3:00 in the morning. I can't wait till the next edition."
**Raymond Outar, Manager—Business Intelligence , Bell Canada**

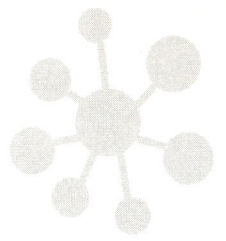

# How The Top 5% Think!

## Principles Of Great Leaders™

### Fred Sarkari

Zal Publishing

Published by BurmanBooks Inc.
260 Queens Quay West
Suite 904
Toronto, Ontario
Canada M5J 2N3

Distribution:
Trumedia Group
c/o Ingram Publisher Services
14 Ingram Blvd.
LaVergne, TN 37086

ISBN 978-1-897404-19-5

Printed in Canada

# Contents

# Dedicated To The Two People I Respect Most In Life

It is truly amazing how we get to where we want to be in life. What influences, inspires, and continually pushes us to achieve greatness even when the task seems over-whelmingly impossible? For me this source of inspiration has always been my parents. Their guidance and unwavering support has motivated me to always do my very best and to help others. To me they are great leaders.

My parents have made so many sacrifices for my sister and I. They gave up a life of material and emotional comforts in India and migrated to Canada, so that my sister and I could have every opportunity to attend the best schools and have the best jobs. In essence, so we would never do without. We did have access to these opportunities in India; however, my parents thought that it would be easier for us to take advantage of them by being a part of the westernized society. They were right.

Their constant love and devotion is the reason I am who I am today. They gave me the freedom to make my own mistakes, but they have always been there to provide me with support and direction. They bestowed upon me more than what I needed and showered me with love and compassion.

My parents are the kind of people that would give anyone the shirt off of their back in order to help. I aspire to follow their teachings, as one of the most valuable lessons that they have taught me is to always have *good thoughts, say good words and do good deeds.*

I have never heard my parents complain.

My father worked sixty hours a week to provide for us. His loyalty to his family and his belief in self-improvement awarded him with the determination to go to night school for seven years to study engineering. This was in addition to him taking care of his family.

For many years my mother worked in an office environment that did not allow her to flourish. However, she did not complain. She worked there in order to ensure that her children had a chance of attaining a successful life. Her unwavering devotion and compassion are two of the most marvelous things that I have ever borne witness to.

Dad, you taught me how to persevere in the face of adversity. Your loyalty and benevolence to our family has been nothing short of inspirational.

Mom, your splendid beauty and brightness touch all who are in your presence. If more people in this world had your level of commitment and compassion, it would be a better place.

I have heard many people say, "I never want to be like my parents." I guess I am one of the fortunate few that do. If I can follow in both of your footsteps, and live my life with the devotion and integrity that you have taught me, then I know that I will have lived a life full of love and purpose; the life of a great man!

Thank you for the sacrifices you have made. Thank you for believing in me and inspiring me to be who I am today.

I love you.

*TO MY SISTER:*

Kashmira, you are one of the most focused and disciplined people that I have ever known. You once told me, "pay now and play later; or play now and pay later, it's your choice. If you make the right choices, you can live the life that you en-vision for yourself." You were right. Thank you for being an example of focus and dedication. You never lost sight of what you wanted and today you are an accomplished doctor, wife, and mother because of it. Thank you and Zubin for one of the greatest gifts ever given to me—the title of Uncle. The birth of my niece Natasha and nephew Zal, truly changed my outlook on life and has further opened up my heart.

# ACKNOWLEDGEMENT

This book has been over two years in the making; there were times when I could not see an end in sight. Thank you to everybody who encouraged and supported me along the way, you've all guided me back to my path when I felt I'd lost my direction.

To all my friends and loyal clients, thank you for all your support, for all your encouragement and for never making me feel that I was not capable of finishing this book. I was able to keep focused and complete something that is a part of my vision; to leave behind *a legacy of compassion.*

Throughout the course of my life, I have read many books, sat through many seminars, and been involved in many engaging conversations with people from all walks of life. Some of these conversations have transformed my personal theories and opinions.

I would like to thank all those who, at one time or another, shared their stories with me. They have made a world of difference as to how I think, the choices I make and in turn the life that I live.

I hope that these stories impact those that I share them with as much as they impacted me.

# DNA OF THE TOP 5%

1 Embrace Change

2 Link Choices to Desired Outcome

7 Invest In Yourself

DNA of the Top 5%

6 Be Aware of Your Perceptions

3 Keep your commitments

5 Focus On Your Goals

4 Be Willing To Fail

# LEADERSHIP FOR LIFE

We all have relationships with people in our personal and professional lives where we provide guidance and/or exert influence. Often within these interactions, we assume leadership roles but do not perform the duties required of a leader. In order to cultivate a mutually satisfying relationship, you need to be able to apply principles of leadership.

## THE IMPORTANCE OF
## CULTURE IN AN OFFICE

The 7 Principles of Great Leaders grants us an awareness of the way that all great leaders think. It provides insight into the fact that it is not a product or service that these leaders provide that makes them successful. It is how they think. Thinking is what keeps them consistent in all aspects of their life. It is a philosophy that is unshakable. This philosophy is backed by the 7 Principles of Great Leaders that you will encounter in this book.

If you want to create an operative culture in your office it is a necessity for you to understand the impact of these principles and to instill it in every single one of your employees.

If you want to be a better sales person, employee, manager and above all, a great leader, understanding these principles are a necessary task. As well, understanding how great leaders have applied these principles is a key contributing factor to your future success.

## TAKING YOUR BUSINESS
## TO THE NEXT LEVEL

If you own your business and want to take it to the next level, you need to adopt the philosophies and principles that all great leaders live by.

Customers look for true leaders in their industry to trust them with their business. In the absence of true leadership, they have no choice but to do business with whom ever knocks on their door. By implementing these principles in your life and by building your business around them, customers will be knocking on your door wanting to build long lasting and profitable relationships with you.

The 7 Principles of Great Leaders will equip you with direction, passion, and most importantly, purpose in both your professional and personal life, thus giving you the freedom and clarity to seek out the kinds of customers you want and you need to be successful.

## CREATING A MORE FULFILLING
## WORK EXPERIENCE

We cannot always control all of the circumstances that cross our path in life. What we can control is how we respond to these circumstances.

Every circumstance that we face in life, be it at work or home, can prove to be either a positive or negative situation. How we respond to these circumstances, ultimately determines the outcome.

No matter what industry or office we work in, stress is a perpetual factor. Due to stress we often lose focus. By way of our weakened sense of clarity these circumstances take control of our lives. By implementing the 7 Principles of Great Leaders, it will allow you to embrace a greater awareness of your choices towards the circumstances that surround your life.

In order for us to be effective and to enjoy our work, we need to link purpose to all that we do in life. By applying the 7 Principles of Great Leaders to all that we do, the results will transcend into all aspects of your life. By gaining freedom and clarity, you will become a more effective individual.

## BUILDING IN-DEPTH
## RELATIONSHIPS

So often we make the mistake of trying to change those around us. Time and time again these efforts prove to be futile. In order for anyone around you to begin the process of change, the change must first take place within you! All great leaders lead by example. How can you expect something from someone that you yourself do not possess? Remember, you cannot change the world but you do have the ability to change yourself. Then and only then will you notice your world changing, giving us the clarity we need to create the level of relationship that we long for.

## INSTILLING VALUES
## IN OUR CHILDREN

Parenting is one of the most important jobs you'll ever have. At times it will be painful and other times it will bring you more joy than you ever imagined possible. Both challenging and rewarding, it is by far the most fulfilling job in the world. One of the greatest fears parents have is failing their children. With enough love, guidance, and most of all, patience, there can be no failure.

Once you have adopted the 7 Principles of Great Leaders in your life and you see the benefits and positive impacts that it has on you, you will want to share your newfound philosophy with those you love.

One of the greatest pleasures you experience as a parent, is watching your children thrive. You can't be with your children every minute so therefore, you must instill values in them; For example, direction, passion and purpose. Arming them with these simple tools can give them the ability to make good, productive and compassionate decisions along the way.

Children yearn for direction and like little sponges; they soak up information at an astonishing rate. They may question your guidance and may not always agree with you, they may even fight you along the way. Keep in mind that in reality children are always seeking the inner truth. The best way that kids learn is through the example of their parents.

The 7 Principles of Great Leaders will demonstrate how

to give your children the tools they need to find a direction of their own. This in turn will allow them the freedom to be themselves, embrace who they are and discover their own unique personality.

These principles will show you how to equip your children with the necessary strengths and confidence they'll need to handle any circumstance that they're faced with. Keep in mind all kids grow up, so ultimately it is not children that you are raising, but adults in training.

## WHY DO WE BECOME TEACHERS?

The reason we become teachers is to help mold the minds of the future, to make a difference, to instill passion and a desire for learning within our students.

In most cases teachers are over worked and underpaid. They often don't see the results of their efforts and hard work.

Just as parents, teachers can't follow their students out into the real world. What they can do is teach them the principles that can help them think like the great leaders of our time and give them the tools to make the right choices for their future.

The 7 Principles of Great Leaders will drive your students and give them direction, focus, and a genuine purpose connected to their education, that they can apply in the real world.

School taught me many things but it never taught me how to think in the real world. If I had learned these principles in school, I realize now what an advantage I would have had.

I feel very strongly that every high school, college and university student should read this book. To include this in their curriculum will undoubtedly give them an advantage over their peers; awarding them with an effective way of thinking.

Understanding the challenges that great leaders have faced, as well as the philosophies they used to overcome those challenges and adverse circumstances, will ignite a wanting in your students and inspire in them a passion for learning.

# NOTES

# If You Jump Out Of A Plane You Better Pull Your Rip Cord

Just to let you know where I'm coming from; I absolutely love what I do. I believe in it, I'm passionate about it.

As much as this book was a labour of love, I had a lot of fun writing it and discovered that I had a lot more to say than I ever imagined I would. Often times I found that my thoughts were generating much faster than my fingers could type. Loving and believing in what I was doing made writing this book a much longer process than I had ever imagined as well. I hope that you enjoy reading this book and by the end of it, will be able to apply one or more of these principles to your life. These principles were derived from the great leaders of our past and our present. They're modeled after great leaders from all walks of life. They've been proven and they've stood the test of time.

One of my objectives with this book is to plant a seed in

your mind, which in time will grow to create balance in your life. In this fast paced world it's so easy to lose our balance. What is drawn from this book will be different for each and every reader. For some readers, the seed may flourish today; for others, it will flourish in a few months or gradually over a few years. One thing we must begin to realize is that we are continuously planting seeds, whether good or bad. We're planting seeds in our businesses, in the minds of our customers, and into every aspect of our lives. We must realize that these seeds may not immediately flourish, but may require care and cultivating to flourish fully.

There may be an idea, a line you read in a book, a word you hear in a conversation, or an experience you encounter at a conference that will undoubtedly change the way you look at your life and the way you think in your relationships. Our job is to find that line and to identify that defining moment when it presents itself. Unfortunately most people will never have the pleasure, because most people do not chase that line or keep their minds open to receive it.

> *"If your mind is not open,*
> *an opportunity could hit you on the side of your head*
> *and all you would do is complain about the pain."*

Imagine if you will: you've decided to try your hand at parachuting . . . jumping out of a plane. You invest a day of your life and approximately $300 in this adventure. The morning you arrive in the hangar, you go through mandatory pre-jump training. For instance, how and when to pull the rip cord, what to do; what not to do; what to expect etc. . . .

That afternoon you go up in the plane. It's that point in

time where you must decide to jump out and not be pushed. There always comes a time in our lives that we have to be accountable for what we want to achieve. Now back to the plane. You've invested your day and your hard earned money, you have the training required to jump successfully, but for whatever reason the moment you jump, you refuse to pull the rip cord. How useful is that chute to you now?

This is exactly how the human mind works. If we open it, it has potential beyond our wildest dreams, but if left unopened it is useless.

I challenge you to jump in and read about the 7 Principles of Great Leaders with an open mind. Reflect upon these principles and how they can be applied to your everyday life. Keep in mind, leadership is not about changing others, it is about inspiring others and living a life of purpose. While through our example, giving others value and direction. It's about having the courage to change yourself.

*"Leadership is about living a life of purpose"*

# NOTES

# How The Top 5% Think!
## 7 Principles Of Great Leaders

L
ooking back, I can recall having a conversation with a close friend regarding the ever-elusive 'Top 5%.' Who or even what would be considered to be the Top 5%? Is it a financial, a physical, or a spiritual goal?

I have pondered the idea of whether or not being financially free would make me a member of the Top 5%. Would an Olympic athlete be considered part of the Top 5%? Does a Buddhist Monk who has attained enlightenment qualify for the Top 5%?

Ultimately, what I started to discover was that those in the 'Top 5%' in any aspect of life, whether it be business, personal, or spiritual, each has a consistent way of thinking.

Our focus shouldn't be the differences in their circumstances or the nature of their unique successes; instead the focus should be on the consistent way they choose to respond to their individual situations. Their response to what surrounds them is what makes them unique, it is what makes them part of the Top 5%. Simply put, the wealth is not in what they can achieve but instead in the way that they consistently think and respond in every aspect of their lives. This is what makes them successful.

The Top 5% have learned that actions will always be determined by a given thought process. Focus on your daily thoughts and your actions will surely follow.

Throughout this book we will focus on seven realistic principles that everyone will encounter within the course of their lives. The goal behind focusing on these principles is to better understand how the Top 5% would respond to them daily in their own lives as a method of creating success.

Principle 1: Embrace Change
Principle 2: Link Choices to Desired Outcome
Principle 3: Keep Your Commitments
Principle 4: Be Willing to Fail
Principle 5: Focus on Your Goals
Principle 6: Be Aware of Your Perceptions
Principle 7: Invest in Yourself

### 1. Embrace Change

There is only one constant in life and that is *change*. No matter how hard you try, you cannot prevent change, so embracing it is your best option. As humans we tend to fear the unknown. The result of *change,* more often than not, is unpredictable and that scares most of us. We try to avoid *change* rather than accept it; this is common. In order to accept *change* and spin it in our favour we must first make the conscious decision (choic*e*) to embrace it.

## 2. Link Choices to Desired Outcome

First we make our *choices;* then our *choices* make us.

There are probably very few people in this world that can honestly say they have never heard a phrase similar to "You made your bed, now you've got to lie in it." It is difficult to argue the fact that as long as we have freedom of *choice,* we will have the burdens and blessings of facing the consequences of those *choices.*

In order for our *choices* to become effective, we must commit ourselves to those decisions. How will you *choose* to be different?

## 3. Keep Your Commitments

Are you indifferent to improving your life? Naturally, this would seem like an inappropriate question considering the fact that you've decided to pick up this book. Indifference is not a word that we would use to describe our feelings towards our family but sometimes our actions project an attitude of indifference. The majority of our waking hours are spent thinking about or participating in our careers, yet there is always something about our 'jobs' that we just do not like.

Your *commitment* to your choices will be reflected in what you put forth in your daily activity. As an individual, you have all the authority to make those *changes* in your life. Let the freedom of *choice* be the fuel to your *commitment.*

One must realize that when *choosing* to make a *commitment* there is an element of short-term failure.

### 4. Be Willing to Fail

How do you measure success without *failure?*

To succeed at anything, we have to be willing to first accept that *failure* will exist on our way to success. Neither success nor *failure* is an overnight accomplishment; each equals the sum of our daily activities. Success or *failure* is cumulative over a week . . . a month . . . a year . . . a lifetime. Success can also be the product of an accumulation of *failures.*

As you may now see more clearly, success is a by-product of our way of thinking. It's a philosophy and an approach to life.

### 5. Focus on Your Goals

*Goals* give you direction and when these goals are met; you get a feeling of accomplishment and material proof of your progress.

One thing to keep in mind is that we will always end up, where we put our focus. *Goals* help us maintain our focus. They're our road map leading us in the direction of our desired destination. *Goals* are a means of incrementally measuring our success.

### 6. Be Aware of Your Perceptions

Whether a *perception* is born out of higher education or a simple lighthearted story shared at a dinner party; each one of us interprets what we hear differently. We've all encountered the concept of "mind-over-matter." The situations that we find ourselves in can be enough to change our entire outlook, depending on our *perception.* We really can control the power of our minds. Certainly not by coincidence, when we focus our energy on the negative, we are consequently planting the seeds of negativity in our lives.

One of the most unfortunate things to witness is someone who has a false *perception* of unrealistic expectations they've set for themselves. In turn they feel that their goals are unattainable. A downward spiral of frustration usually ensues and they become overwhelmed and discouraged until eventually what started with good intentions and promise ends in frustration and anger.

Minor changes in our *perception* will lead us to desirable outcomes. Naturally, the *choices* that we make are largely based on what we think is best for us, given our unique set of circumstances. It is our *perception* of the circumstances that will dictate the *choices* we make. By closely monitoring our *perceptions* (right, wrong or indifferent) we can start to better control our *choices* and in turn control whether or not we attain our desired success. In this chapter we're going to take a deeper look at the *perceptions* we've applied to our lives, careers our circumstances, etc. As well, we'll take a look at the ways these *perceptions* can affect us and how we can use them to our advantage.

### 7. Invest in Yourself

Do you remember the story about the Three Little Pigs? Straw, sticks and bricks were the materials they used to build their houses. The materials that went into each of those little houses directly influenced their capacity to withstand the forces of the Big Bad Wolf.

"Garbage in . . . Garbage out . . ." what you invest in yourself, is what you'll get out of yourself . . . Sounds simple, doesn't it? Imagine you were given a house to live in for free. Upon getting your new residence you learn that it's the last house you'll ever have and it's expected to last you for the rest of your life. Would you invest in keeping that house sound? Would you ensure that it stood on a solid foundation? How about its appearance? What if that residence was your body? You need to live in it for the rest of your life. What is your 'spring-cleaning' agenda? What are you constructing your foundation from, to ensure that it is sound?

We are a product of the environment we create for ourselves. Some elements of that environment may be beyond our control, yet we can always control the development of our character. Ask yourself, "What can I do to start improving myself today?"

We will take a closer look at the 7 Principles of Great Leaders and how the success of applying these principles made a great impact in their lives. I should point out to you that throughout the course of this book, you will see that the 7 Principles are most effective when used in conjunction with each other. Don't get me wrong; individually, each principle holds it's own, but when applied in combination with each other, and applied to every aspect of your life, the possibilities are truly endless.

# NOTES

# Strength Of A Leaders Character

*"Leadership is never easy but very simple. What we have to do in order to be an effective leader is simple; doing it takes a lot of effort."*

Visiting the doctor's office always seems to start the same way for me. It begins with a hurried rush to get there with enough time to prepare for my wait. On one occasion, I was sitting patiently in the waiting room when I came across a tattered copy of a Canadian business magazine. This particular issue must have been fairly well written judging by the number of pages that had been dog-eared. These are the moments in life where curiosity grabs a hold of me and for whatever reason I want to know what others have found so interesting. As I flipped through the creased pages I came across an article on New Year's resolutions for effective sales people. Being an inquisitive sales professional, I started to scour the article and I found that the points that were made were quite impressive and practical in nature. Some of the items were so pragmatic that I was exclaiming to myself "Wow, this is something that I could be doing when I get back to the office!"

My mind started racing as I began to think of ways to incorporate this newly acquired information into my sales arsenal. My eyes darted back and forth across each bulleted item, looking for more and more tools to take back with me. Then it hit me. A sudden, stimulating realization: "You know this already!"

Have you ever had a similar experience? Given all the articles that you've read, seminars that you've attended, and sessions that you've facilitated, have you ever been re-introduced to something from your past, that you'd misplaced in your mind? That when re-connected, you found it so rejuvenating to your career or personal life that it made you laugh to yourself at its simplicity?

There are no new ways of thinking that successful industry leaders have created on their own. These ideas and thoughts have been around for centuries. The only difference is that few are willing to continue on with what is required in order to reap the benefits and see the results from these ideas. Following through with implementing them in our lives is typically the falling off point for most of us.

Take a moment to think about the times that you walked through a crowd. When you see someone walking down the street or perhaps even just sitting in one spot, can you tell from just one glance if he or she is a leader? Is this person the head of a powerful organization, a top sales producer, or a team motivator? The answer is no. Leadership is not a physical trait and can't be discerned through physical examination. Leadership is largely part of a mental trait that conditions the actions and attitudes of the leader.

Strength of character is derived from philosophies comprised of distinctive traits that leaders possess. Traits such as desire, direction, values, passion and purpose provide such a distinction. In turn, these traits provide them with the strength, confidence, and courage to effectively respond to their unique circumstances. This is the philosophy of the Top 5%, of the great leaders of all time.

Strength of character is infectious, motivational and above all, inspires loyalty and commitment in team members. Strength of character is the stuff that can help you get the most out of each and every team member, by leading through example and instilling the correct traits in them. Remember that anyone can hold the title of leader, but the leaders that get the most out of their teams are those that earn the respect and admiration of team members. A strong character is one sure way to get that respect and admiration. The strength of a leader's character is determined by what they do every day to lead themselves.

The importance of character is illustrated in the use of the phrase "Ace" in the Air Force. Military analysts have always been amazed at the confidence, skill level, and results of their "Aces." These analysts show that "Aces" account for approximately 5% of the air force and have an amazing 80% success rate on missions. They attribute this incredible success rate to the character traits of the people that become "Aces." This elite group of fighters bring such an incredible combination of desire, direction, focus, passion, and purpose that they literally will themselves to succeed and in doing so encourage, motivate and lead their teams to continually improve their performance.

Examine your own leadership. Do you possess strength of

character? Are you the "Ace" that leads your team? Will your team members follow your lead quickly, passionately and at 110%? To continue to be effective, you will have to answer yes to all of the above questions.

*"The strength of a leaders character is dictated by what he / she does everyday to lead themselves."*

# NOTES:
What is the one thing you have taken away from this chapter?

# Don't Fight The Process

Wwhat comes to mind when I say "McDonald's"? Does the name conjure up images of effervescent, pony-tailed teens asking if you'd like fries with that? Definitely! What else? Do you think healthy?

Most people I talk to, don't. However, you may have noticed that for the last couple of years McDonalds has spent millions of dollars and countless man hours, creating a healthier food menu.

People make decisions based on the perceptions we've left behind for them. A new-country song that I heard on the radio presents a scenario of four people meeting an untimely death in a motor vehicle accident, yet only three grave markers were visible. Grimm, yes, but the message to me was clear . . . not that the fourth individual had left a negative impression behind but that the impression left was perhaps not as positive as it could have been. Of course, that is just a song and the artists of our day can easily string words together to paint any picture of their choosing, but the fact does remain that we make decisions based on the perceptions that we have. And that's something we're going to talk about in one of the following chapters.

Do you think it's inexpensive for what you get in a McDonald's meal? In order to have a full meal it will cost you approximately ten dollars Canadian, so why is it, that it costs up to $1,030,500 U.S. to start up a new McDonald's franchise location, and then have to enroll in 'Hamburger University' for training? (11)

Is it not just easier to exercise your other choice and set up a Ma & Pa burger joint for $150,000? Why such a drastic margin? Especially when most would agree that the burgers at the Ma & Pa joints taste better, and are less expensive. You see, when you spend the much higher price for the McDonald's and go to Hamburger University you are not attending in order to learn to push burgers. You are learning a process; that's what you're paying for. $1M and a $45,000 franchise fee for a winning process, a process that the men and women at McDonald's have been trying to perfect since the sixties.

It's important to start recognizing and understanding that everything we do in our business and our lives is a process . . . everything. Now, that doesn't mean we're using an effective process, or even if it is an effective process, it doesn't mean it couldn't be more effective.

If the effectiveness of our process is so crucial to our success, we should ask ourselves what kind of processes the Top 5% are following? What are McDonald's and Tim Horton's doing in the "Quick Service Industry" that makes them part of the Top 5%? This book is not about their strategies but instead it is about their way of thinking. In essence, find the top 5% in what you want to achieve, and learn about their daily thought process.

The question we need to ask ourselves every day is "What is our process?" Let me ask you this; When you wake up in the morning, do you have to think about brushing your teeth or do you just do it? This mentality transcends into every aspect of our daily lives; how we speak, how we think, how we lead our lives and how we lead others.

What are our processes when dealing with co-workers? What process do we employ when it comes to our personal lives and relationships? Awareness precedes effective change. We need to become aware of our present situation before we can effectively make any changes in our lives.

Another thing to remember is that no matter how strong your processes are, it's important to understand that we are dealing with human beings that have feelings and emotions. Can you carve anything in stone when dealing with people? No, you cannot. Due to people's emotions every situation will be observed with at least minor differences. That is why our processes need to be customized to accommodate different people's situations, while keeping the foundation of our processes consistent. Therefore, what you read in this book is what has worked for the great leaders of our time. What you need to do is take these ideas and mold them to who you are, to your professional and personal relationships, and to your environment. Your task is simple: understand your process, figure out what you need to do to make it more effective, mold it to yourself and then continue that evolution to meet the needs of your customers and others around you.

What are you trying to accomplish in your relationships and industry? If your primary focus is to make more money, then you should not be in business. If your number one reason is to get more deals to grow your business, increase your clientele, or get more referrals, you should not be in business, as you will not be as effective as you can be. Lindsay Owen Jones, chairman of L'Oreal, one of the fastest and the largest growing cosmetic company in the world was asked in an interview, "What's the reason for your success?" His response was "We love this industry and our customers, just a little more than our competition." What we have to start to do is become more aware of the people that we deal with and become more aware of our customers' needs. That should be the motivating factor. What is it we're trying to accomplish for them? What legacy are we going to leave for them? When you begin focusing on your customers and trying to help them get what they want, the referrals will follow. In turn, money will come, your business will grow and most importantly, your relationships will grow exponentially.

This way of thinking should be consistent throughout both your personal and professional life. The focus should be on helping people get what they want and in turn, your return on investment will be higher than ever imagined.

*"If the effectiveness of our process is so crucial to our success, we should ask ourselves what kind of a process the Top 5% are following?"*

## NOTES:
Who are the Top 5% in your industry, profession, etc.?  Why?

# What I Learned From My Niece And Nephew

*"In order to understand leadership at its essence,
take lessons from a child."*

Parents will agree that children are the greatest gifts in the world. Children are the greatest joys of our lives and yes at times, they could also bring the greatest stress into our lives. I have a beautiful 9-year-old niece and 7-year-old nephew. They absolutely love life. Natasha and Zal have demonstrated to me how children come to us more evolved than adults. Kids are the ones that remind us of the lessons we need to learn in life.

The material items that children receive in their lives have very little to do with what makes them truly happy. Now, that's not to say that my niece and nephew are content playing with pocket lint, but at such a young age it becomes clear what they genuinely care about. Laughter, hugs and kisses seem to perpetuate their happiness. They are really not concerned with the trivial things that occur around them everyday. Sure spilling something brings that ominous look of concern to their face but why does that happen? Because they know that the adults in the room are going to be displeased with them. Adults are the ones that focus on such trivial matters. It is amazing how we let something as small as "spilled milk" ruin a good portion of our day.

There are tragic stories of life lost at very young ages. People who have gone through such excruciating tragedy would welcome spilled milk in a heartbeat. Unfortunately, in order to appreciate the little things in life it often takes a dramatic turn of events to open our eyes and admire the simplicity of the things that we so often take for granted.

"Children come to us more evolved than adults in order to teach us the lessons we need to learn in life"(15). Many years ago, I heard this powerful statement. It was one of those statements that's never left my mind and more so my heart.

It was one of those times that my mind and heart was open to it and therefore, it changed how I thought on a daily basis. It's astonishing how when our minds are not open to knowledge and growth, an opportunity can hit us in the back of our head and all we'll do is complain about the pain.

What is the number one question children ask? "WHY?" How powerful is that question? It may annoy many of us when children continually ask it, but what we need to do is to learn from them. We need to start asking ourselves these *why* questions:

*Why* are companies doing business with us?

*Why* aren't they doing business with us?

*Why* do we get the referrals we do?

*Why* don't we get the referrals we want?

If we don't ask *why,* we are not going to be aware of our present situation. If we don't know our present situation, we can't maintain effective changes. By asking *why,* we become more aware of our surroundings, our perception of things, and the situations we tend to find ourselves in.

I've been guilty of this, and I have seen many people be guilty of this as well. I have close friends who have young children. Whenever I visit their homes it's amazing to see how happy and content their children are. Their children laugh and smile constantly. On the opposite end of the spectrum, I have visited homes where I've said to myself, "That kid does nothing but cry and scream, never smiles never laughs." So we brand kids, do we not? At specific points in time we brand them and their personalities. We brand them based on their consistent actions and we brand them based on what emotions they have left stirred up within us.

### *"By asking why, we become more aware of our surroundings."*

Is it a fair assumption to say our customers and the people around us brand us as well? But the question is what are they talking about, what are they basing this impression on? What are they saying about you when you go to their office, when you have a conversation over the phone with them, what kind of feelings do you leave behind? Most times when somebody leaves your office you can't remember what he or she said, but you will remember how you felt. You will remember how someone made you feel two years ago, but have no clue what they said one week ago. This is the same thing with our customers; it's the emotions that we leave behind. What makes us different? What kind of emotions are we leaving behind? You see, customers are saying and feeling something. The question is who controls those perceptions? We do. But when we don't focus on controlling their emotions, we give them the right to think and feel what ever they want, and that usually is not to our benefit.

Did you know that the average infant laughs approximately four hundred times a day? How about the average adult; the answer is fifteen times a day. Four hundred times compared to fifteen (14). Take the time right now and just smile, think of something that will make you crack a huge smile. When you think of something that puts a smile on your face, your whole mental state changes, even your body expressions change; it makes you feel energized. Whatever makes you smile and laugh, make sure that you have it in front of your mind at all times.

People that take the simple things in life for granted may sometimes feel that there is nothing to smile about. Our thoughts are powerful. They can determine the outcome of our actions. If our thoughts are negative we tend to react in a negative manner, yet if our thoughts are positive, our responses will also be positive. We are all capable of thinking positively in every situation and that's what we must turn our focus towards.

We need to learn how to enjoy life unconditionally. We need to find the joy in the little things in life. As adults we tend to focus too much on the circumstances that surround our daily lives that we get so caught up in them. We can learn a valuable lesson from children, because they tend to live in the moment. Have you ever noticed that when children are playing, they exude passion in everything they do? They focus solely on what they're doing at that moment in time and are not concerned with the things that surround them. As we mentioned earlier, it's how we look at our circumstances that will determine the outcome of our actions. Let your customers connect to your lighter side as well as your business side; let them see you laugh as this humanizes you. This is a commonality all humans share. When we laugh and have fun, we learn and grow. Consistency is the key, if you are not laughing with your co-workers, customers, with your partner and children, what kind of emotions and perceptions are you leaving behind? If you are not laughing and enjoying all that you do, what purpose does it have anyways? Remember, it's not the circumstances that you are in; it's the way of thinking that you display.

Have you ever tried to negotiate with your child based on logic? If so, what was the outcome? You probably lost. You didn't get what you needed. They probably didn't listen. They likely looked at you as though you had two heads. What we need to understand is, in order to deal with children we need to negotiate with them on an emotional level first. They are emotional creatures and the only way to have a win—win situation with them is to open up their minds based on emotion first and then justify our recommendations based on logic. Logic is absolutely irrelevant unless their minds and hearts are open to it first.

By watching them it becomes more evident that we're emotional creatures not logical ones. We make decisions in life based on emotion and then justify it based on logic. Is there a difference with children and adults? No! "Children come to us more evolved than adults in order to teach us the lessons we need to learn in life" (15). If we were logical creatures we would not buy expensive luxury cars and million dollar homes and then justify it. It just would not make sense. We make these decisions based on emotion and then justify it with logic. "I know the car is $75,000 but look at all the safety features such as air bags, anti lock brakes . . . not to mention it is a very comfortable ride and you know me I love my music and the stereo system in this car is phenomenal." As I am sure you can agree this is not a logical purchase, it was based purely on emotion. The vehicle features made the purchaser feel good when driving it. If you are in the mortgage business, how many people have bought a home they could logically afford? A very small percentage. We make decisions based on emotion and so do our customers.

In the 1998 Warner Bros. put out a film called the "Negotiator," where Kevin Spacey plays the role of an expert negotiator. There is a specific scene in the movie where he is kneeling down outside of a closed door trying to convince a woman to come out. It turns out that this woman is his wife and she's locked herself in the bathroom because their daughter told her that she looked 'big' in the sweater she was wearing. Kevin Spacey realizes the humour and irony in the situation and says "I can convince a terrorist to come down from the Eiffel Tower but I can't convince my own wife to come out of the bathroom." Because he was using logic, no amount of persuasion would convince her to come out. Why? It was emotion that drove her to lock herself in the bathroom in the first place.

> *"We can learn a valuable lesson from children, for they tend to live in the moment. Have you ever noticed when children are playing, they tend to exude passion in all that they do."*

We need to open the minds and hearts of the people we deal with based on emotion and then justify our recommendations based on logic. Logic is only useful if you're dealing with the right person at the right time with the perfect logical statement—how often does that happen? It's been said many times, "People do not care how much you know, until they know how much you care."

# NOTES:

What are some of the life lessons you have learned from children?

# ABILITY VS. DESIRE

*"The Top 5% create the desire to do the things they need to do,*
*when they need to do it, whether they like it or not"*

H ave you ever felt that your life is an unfinished puzzle and that you are constantly searching for the missing piece? I used to have that same feeling. Corporate, business, personal—a piece of the puzzle always seemed to be missing and wouldn't you know it, it was the piece that I really needed to take me to the next level. The most frustrating part about it was that I didn't have the slightest idea what that little piece was, let alone where to find it!

That feeling as though you are 'missing a piece' will happen, but that's not to say that there is no way around it, or even no way to work with the situation at hand. Awareness always precedes effective change. It is imperative that you are aware of your business and your relationships. I do not mean a simple awareness but one that is much deeper than just cursory knowledge. For instance, I'm aware that there is a way to have my word processor automatically create backup copies of my files, but I don't have the slightest idea how to activate that option and worse yet, at the beginning of my writings, I still hadn't activated the feature. My awareness of this option is really just cursory.

The awareness that I speak of encompasses much more. Awareness in this case, is like attentiveness, something that you are involved in regularly.

Awareness precedes effective change because without it, there is no foundation for change. It will require you to always be aware, not on a yearly basis, not on a monthly basis, but on a regular basis. Your awareness can't be developed once a year by attending a course or reading a book. Although seminars and studying can often be catalysts for change, your awareness is what truly fuels it.

There was a little shopping mall in the North Toronto neighborhood where I grew up. As a young child, my Mom used to drag me there whenever she had some shopping to do. There was this one store I remember that sold puzzles. This was a store that I looked so forward to visiting. Almost like clockwork, whenever we walked past that store I would kick, scream, and conjure up every emotion under the sun to get my mother to take me into that store to buy me a puzzle. My efforts were not successful all the time, my mother was far too smart for that . . . but the times that she did give in to my pressure were sheer bliss for me.

My primary objective on getting that puzzle was to be able to look at the picture on the box. I know it sounds strange, but I would look at that image on the box, be it a house, a boat or a car and I would really want to create that end product. All I would focus on was how wonderful this box of irregular shaped cardboard pieces was going to look when it was finished!

How often have we made forecasts at the beginning of each year? How about the new goals that we have and the new visions of what we are going to accomplish? We make these forecasts with our minds stretched because we can see the end result. We get excited about that. What allows us to see beyond any restrictions is visualizing all of the possibilities.

### *"The awareness I am talking about encompasses so much more."*

I would take that puzzle home, clear off my desk, throw all the pieces down, and do the first thing you do when you build a puzzle: begin to work on the outside edges. The edge pieces are often the easiest to find and the easiest to build.

After the frame was assembled I would begin to fill in the body of the puzzle, of course this always took much longer to piece together. Even though it is easiest to group them by color or texture, they really do not go together as quickly as the edge pieces. Of course the excitement would die down and my interest would wane, that is until I catch a glimpse of the puzzle box. If I did not keep looking at the end result, then distractions, frustrations and doubt would enter my mind. Thoughts such as: "well, I better clean my room or my mom will never buy me another puzzle," and "I better go do the dishes or I'll never get another puzzle." These distractions were always there, but my focus was on something else, it was the visualization of the picture on the box. A few weeks would pass and we would find ourselves once again in the mall.

It is probably no surprise that as human beings our minds are wired to look for accomplishments and results. When we achieve positive results in things that we have invested our time in, we get excited. This cycle drives us to want to accomplish more. Simply put, we want more of those positive feelings.

At the beginning of January you are excited about the year ahead. You visualize your accomplishments dancing around in your head. Natural state of mind is to do the things that are easiest. You are doing things that will give you accomplishment and results and it often drives you to do more. Without warning, reality rears its ugly head. These are the times when you have to do something for your business that you are not fond of doing. The efforts that you put in contribute to the overall goal; however, it lacks the romance that it had when the project first started.

How often do we want to change our strategy and make different choices? Is it as soon as the first quarter has ended? Or halfway through the fiscal year? We want to do something perhaps a little more convenient. We start to look, again, for things that will yield instant results. We look for those things that provide immediate gratification. We tend to go back to doing the same things we're used to doing, the same things that are comfortable for us to do, yet we always expect different results.

> *"The Top 5% are successful because they follow through whereas the remaining 95% just get excited."*

The Top 5% are successful because they follow-through regardless of the circumstances, whereas the remaining 95% just get excited. This is precisely why they make the money they do. However, they don't only do these things for the money.

The money is the by-product of their follow-through. Don't get me wrong, I'm not implying that the remaining 95% are not ambitious. However, intentions without implementation are as productive as the proverbial pushing of water up a hill with a rake.

When we are younger we start off with dreams of metaphorically "ruling the world." We feel that we have a greater purpose in life and want to realize it fully. We might not know what it is, but we know that all the pieces are in front of us somewhere. The unfortunate part is that, as time goes on, it starts to get difficult to locate some of the pieces. Decisions need to be made and while some of us keep looking, others begin to give up. Would knowing that the piece was right around the corner have been enough to keep them searching? Probably.

The truth is, most of us choose not to continue. We abandon our dreams and just exist. We start to just go with the flow and follow the mundane motions of the everyday. Do you think I had the ability to finish those puzzles? Certainly I could have. Then what was lacking? Why was I not able to complete the puzzles? There was a lack of desire. More fittingly, since I began taking my visualization off the end result, I started to lose my initial desire and excitement.

> *"When we are younger we start off with dreams of metaphorically ruling the world."*

Can you imagine a puzzle company making a puzzle of a beautiful house beside a lake? But on the box instead of having a picture all they put was in text "this puzzle will give you a beautiful picture of a house beside a lake." How many of those puzzles do you think will sell?

I do not think logic has ever been mistaken as a fuel for desire. We know that the puzzle company would not sell very many puzzles if all they put on the box were text. Nothing could be more obvious. Why is it then, that we think we can go into our customers' offices and negotiate based on logic and expect them to get excited about working with us? Our customers are more educated than ever, and sometimes it seems like they know more about our industry then we do.

What could you possibly tell them that they don't already know? We need to open up their minds and hearts based on emotions and visualizations and then justify our reasons based on logic.

**"Intentions without implementation are as productive as pushing the proverbial water up a hill with a rake."**

What we need to do is instill more desire in the hearts of our customers. More desire in the hearts of our co-workers and more desire in the hearts of those who we have personal relationships with. Give them all reasons and purpose to pursue the life they have always wanted.

Roger Banister is not exactly a household name, yet in 1954 he created history by breaking a world record. Roger Banister ran one mile in three minutes and 59.4 seconds. That doesn't mean as much in comparison to the athletes of today. The competitive high school athlete can run a mile in four minutes. It's not easy, but it's possible for the committed. Back then however, doctors, physiologists, and psychiatrists all believed the body could not physically endure what was required to complete one mile in four minutes. So, no one tried. By the end of 1957, sixteen other runners broke the four minute mile mark, including John Landy, who did it just forty six days later (20).

How often do we have these visions in our minds? A new idea, or a new strategy that no one else has tried in our industry. An idea so real we know deep inside it could work. Yet we don't follow through with it because no one else has done it. Instead, we say to ourselves "Why bother? It's not going to work anyway."

When Banister set the record, he was asked how he had accomplished this feat no one had ever accomplished before; something that people believed was impossible. He responded by pointing out that before he physically trained for it, he had to mentally train for it. He had to visualize the fact that he could break that record. He had to believe it in his heart first and then when he did that, when that mental training was over, the physical training was less challenging and became the easiest part.

*"Always remember, you will never be greater than your thoughts and therefore we need to nurture our thoughts."*

What he talked about was the balance between one's ability and one's perceived desire. Those who have been involved in any kind of competitive sport, can easily answer whether or not it's comfortable and fun waking up at four or five in the morning to train for a couple hours while everybody else is sleeping? The answer is no. It most certainly is not. However, this is what needs to be done day in and day out to accomplish your best. It becomes crucial to build that desire in your heart so you can feel it and visualize it every day. Up until that pivotal moment, the circumstances can easily overpower your ability to succeed. Every individual reading this book has the potential to be the very best in their industry, the Top 5%. Do you have the desire to commit to be the best?

Each person will receive the messages shared in this book differently. What I took away from Banister's message is that everything happens twice in our lives. Correct me if I'm wrong; in the foundation of how the mind works, you cannot physically do anything, without it being a thought first. It's as simple as that. The question I ask you is: *What do you think about on a daily basis? What goes through your mind about your industry? What goes through your mind about your clients and co-workers? What goes through your mind about your personal relationships?"*

Always remember, you will never be greater than your thoughts. Therefore we need to carefully nurture our thoughts.

Take the time to ask yourself:

Can you be a greater person?
What do you need to do in order to make it a reality?
Can you be a better parent?
What do you need to do in order to make it a reality?
Can you serve your clients better?
Can you be a happier person?
Can you make more money?
What do you need to do in order to make these realities?

You have to start by changing the way you envision these goals. Determine if what you are pursuing can even be categorized as one of your personal goals. You must start to take the steps necessary to change the way you think on a daily basis. These realizations are rarely discovered when it's most convenient. Your growth is dependent on your ability to alter the way in which you envision yourself, your job, and your path.

Nurture your thoughts; your thoughts will determine your outcome. Each one of us has the ability to formulate our own thoughts. We can choose to approach situations from many different angles.

> *"Nurture your thoughts; your thoughts will*
> *determine your outcome."*

Let's talk about our customer, John Doe. John Doe represents the one customer that we need to keep on the roster because he's a good customer as far as volume is concerned. One of those customers that even provides you with good referrals, but for whatever personal reasons, you just can't bring yourself to deal with him on a regular basis. Sound familiar? Sure, we all have them. How often do we make the mistake by saying things like "I have to go see John today but I don't want to"? I will sit there and I will pace in my office—"I have to go see John, he gives me grief every time I go see him." Then we start vocalizing this, and we start sharing it with everyone around us, "do you know I have to go see John today? Do you know what he does to me, yeah, he ruins my whole day." It has nothing to do with me it has everything to do with John. "But I have to go see him anyway because he brings me good business."

Do you think I could be more effective going to see John with more positive thoughts? Absolutely! Yet, how often do we make this mistake?

Rarely is the question ever about ability. Everyone reading this book has the ability to do what they want in his or her own lives. The question is do you have the desire to do the things 95% of the people are not willing to do? Without ever crossing any ethical boundaries, would you do what you need to if you knew that it would separate you from the pack and secure your position amongst the top 5%?

It's of the utmost importance that we simplify our lives and thought processes. We need to get back to the basics. We need to allow our minds to go back to a time of innocence and exuberance, back to a time when there were a thousand times more challenges in life than burdens. We need to bring out the child within us.

On May 23, 1984, this remarkable story was carried over the wires of the Associated Press. "As a child, Mary Groda was unable to learn to read and write. Educational experts labeled her as retarded. In her adolescent years she was given an additional label, incorrigible, and was sentenced to two years in a reformatory. Ironically, it was inside the oppressive confines of the reformatory that Mary would rise to the challenge of learning. By working hard at her studies, sometimes as long as sixteen hours per day, she earned her GED.

> **"The question is do you have the desire to do the things 95% of the people are not willing to do?"**

A stream of unfortunate circumstances would visit Mary Groda. Upon leaving the reformatory, she became pregnant outside of wedlock. Two years later a second pregnancy would come about, this one resulted in her having a devastating stroke. One which resulted in the radical loss of her memory and all the skills she had worked so hard to achieve. With the help and support of her father, Mary worked hard to regain what she had lost. In serious financial straits, Mary was forced to accept welfare. In order to make ends meet, she took in seven foster children. It was during this period that she started taking courses at a community college. Upon completion of her coursework she applied to and was accepted by a medical school. In the spring of 1984 Mary Groda-Lewis (now married) paraded in full academic regalia across the graduation stage. That day the woman that was once labeled as retarded and incorrigible received another label, this time a degree listing her as Mary Groda-Lewis, M.D." (7)

This does not mean that Mary Groda-Lewis is in the Top 5% of all physicians. Mary Groda-Lewis had developed a level of desire required to overcome her personal circumstances and create success.

During the times in our life when we feel there is no light, we create the labels we allow ourselves to live under. Anyone can make the right decisions when circumstances are optimal. The true test of character; perseverance and vision is demonstrated when we make the right decisions under difficult circumstances.

When difficult circumstances intrude on our lives, some people quit, complain and resign themselves to living under those conditions, accepting their unhappiness and dissatisfaction. Others tend to struggle and fight for their vision and never give up, regardless of how insurmountable their current conditions appear. Certainly, there is a difference between those who fail and those who succeed when facing hardship. The difference, however, is not one of education, background, support system, skills or intelligence, but instead of desire. It's the level of desire that burns inside someone in order to fight through pain and adversity, of doing what others are not willing to do. Passion is extreme, it is compelling, and it is an intense emotional driver. In order to keep the flame of desire lit within you, you must have passion. Passion is the fuel, and desire is the fire.

Desire is one of the main character traits which lead to success. If you want to be in the Top 5%, you have to develop a higher level of desire, you have to be willing to do what the Top 5% do. If you commit yourself to performing the same activities as 95% of the people around you, then you can expect to receive what 95% of the people receive.

The truth is that the world is filled with people who have had to deal with the utmost of life's challenges, and they have emerged victorious. It's your desire, passion and purpose that will allow you to endure what you need to, including going through the pain and suffering in order to get what you want out of life.

*Ask yourself this,*
*"Would the child you once were, be proud of the*
*adult that you have become?"(15)*

# NOTES:

List 10 desires that at one point in your life burned within you.

# DNA OF THE TOP 5%

**1**
Embrace Change

DNA of the Top 5%

# The Nail Just Does Not Hurt Bad Enough
## Embrace Change

*"The secret of every man who has ever been successful*
*lies in the fact that he formed the habit of doing things*
*that failures don't like to do."*
*Dr. Gray an executive of the Prudential Insurance Company said*
*in his speech "The Common Denominator of Success."*

One of the greatest books I have ever read is the 'Art of War' by Sun Tzu. Sun Tzu was a war strategist. His writings and strategies from 2,500 years ago are widely used in many aspects of the business world today. Sun Tzu said, "Imagine a boulder perched on top of a hill, although temporarily stabilized it has great potential power."(17) The moral of that story is that even though the boulder has great power it is absolutely useless if it is not pushed over the hill.

Once we push ourselves over that hill all we need to do is direct that momentum. Every single individual has potential power beyond their wildest dreams, unfortunately only 5% of us are willing to explore anywhere beyond our own center of gravity. The step required in order to establish momentum toward success. Is your life like that large boulder on the edge of a hill?

*What do you suppose is holding you back?*

### *"I was sick and tired of just existing, feeling like a dead fish floating down stream."*

We all have great potential beyond our wildest dreams—what we need to do is become aware of what is holding us back. The boulder requires gravity's insistent pull in order to accomplish the descent downhill. As an example, in the absence of gravity, the boulder would have no fuel with which to descend the hill. We too require fuel, only our trip is constantly ascending. Our ascent to the realm of the Top 5% needs to be fueled. Countless times in the past, I could easily dislodge myself from my perch, but the momentum I required was never to be found. We need to leverage that which we are sick and tired of. It is that frustration that can fuel our desire.

A short story might illustrate my thoughts more clearly:

It was only a couple of years ago that I realized what I was sick and tired of in my life? My awakening came from the feelings I had from people trying to control my life. Telling me what to do, what not to do, what I was capable of doing and what I was not . . . it all had to stop. Time was one of my hottest commodities . . . everyone has it, no one owns it yet we continue to invest it and I for one rarely received any returns. I was tired of people controlling my time. I was sick and tired of watching my parents work so hard with integrity and passion in their family's best interest yet still having others seemingly in control. I was weary of realization that the little I was doing was not making an impact in people's lives; scared of not leaving a legacy behind for anyone. I was sick and tired of just existing, feeling like a dead fish floating down stream.

It's absolutely crucial to know what more it is that you want in life. We have to stop the pattern of existence. If we are not growing we are falling behind. But we never stay constant; we either go forward or we fall back, but we never stay the same.

Now, as you can tell, I get a little passionate about this. This is not a speech, it comes from within. I hope my sincerity will be the stepping-stone for your change, the catalyst to start exploring yourself beyond your center of gravity.

> Ask yourself; is there anything you would like to change in your life? Take a moment and write down the first thing that comes to your mind.

The kinetic energy of that boulder exists. To put it into action requires two key things.

1- A catalyst for change,
2- Fuel to maintain momentum.

You want to unleash your potential because you feel as though you are leashed. What is holding you back? Is it your circumstances? No. It is the way you THINK about your circumstances? By making some simple changes daily, you can change the direction and quality of your entire life.

First and foremost, we need to stop dwelling on the past. One of the first steps to accomplishing great things in your life is to cease dwelling on the negative things in your past. Carefully assess your present strengths, successes, and achievements. Embrace those positive events in your life and quit limiting your potential by constantly thinking about what you may have done poorly.

> *"Every single individual has potential beyond their wildest dreams."*

Never allow the past to hinder you, instead, let it be part of your future. Allow those past adversities to be part of your growth. No matter how hard you try, you can't prevent change. Embracing change is your best option. In order to change anything in your life you must first be aware of your present state. You must know where you are and where you want to go.

What frustrates you in your current situation?

Take the time to look within yourself.

What do you like and dislike about who you have become?

Look into the future to see who you want to become and who you do not want to become?

After you are aware of the above, then and only then can you make the necessary changes.

Many people will sit there and hope things will change. If I want things to change in my life then I have to do something different. If you want something different in your life, you have to be willing to do something different. How simple is that?

I became a student of knowledge . . . a student of success. I have been to many seminars and read countless books. I have spent numerous hours listening to tapes regarding business and personal relationships. I always try to focus on picking up something that could potentially change my life . . . for this makes it all worthwhile. Now I say potentially, because it depends if my mind is open to suggestion and if I'm willing to commit to the choices that I would need to, in order to start understanding and gaining that knowledge.

Is knowledge power? No. Knowledge is 'potential' power just like the boulder on top of the hill. After a while I was able to find my boulder, but I still had to gain the desire, the reason, and purpose to topple it from its perch.

The question that needed to be answered was: am I willing to do what the average is not willing to do? In order for me to reach the Top 5%, was I willing to do what the 5% does or was I going to revert to doing what the 95% still do? Was I willing to commit to the principles at the same level that the great leaders have committed to throughout history?

*"If I wanted things to change in my life then I had to do something different in my life."*

Oddly enough, what took me a while to understand was that the Top 5% *were* willing to do the things that the 95% were *not* willing to. It's not that 95% can't do the things the Top 5% do, it's that the remaining 95% would not be as willing to pay the long-term price, thus perching another proverbial boulder on yet another hill. The main difference between the

5% and the 95% was the way that they consistently thought and approached their daily state of affairs in every situation surrounding their lives. Their state of mind is their number one priority.

Knowing and still not doing, is in a sense, not truly knowing. There could be some allowance for one who is truly blind to a situation because without being aware they certainly can't know. Most simply don't want to know and turn a blind eye. For acknowledging something renders you accountable. What then becomes of those who know and still choose to be ignorant? There are no allowances for those who know yet choose not to follow-through.

If you truly knew how the results could change your life, would you make the changes that are required in order to progress? When you feel it in the core of your heart then it will be a lot easier to commit to the changes.

If we agree that the one constant in life is change, then why do we have such a hard time accepting change in our lives? Why do we have such a hard time changing the mentality of our customers to want to do business with us instead of doing it with our competition? Why is that so difficult? Why is it so difficult to change the little things in our life when we know what to do? It is our fear of the unknown that tends to hold us back from accepting change. Newton once said, "for every action, there is an equal or opposite reaction." The fact is that we can't always foresee every reaction—to us this is the ever-fearful unknown.

We're all creatures of habit—most of what we do is derived from a habit that we have been nurturing and relied on for years. Right from how we brush our teeth to how we deal with our customers and other relationships. It's important to note that there are many ways of accomplishing the things we want. We can do whatever we want, however we want, but are all the things we do beneficial? Are the habits that you've developed completely beneficial to you, your business, and your family?

A piece from "I am your constant companion" has stayed in my office for many years:

*Take me, train me, be firm with me*
*And I will place the world at your feet.*
*Be easy with me and I will destroy you.*
*Who am I?*
*I am Habit.*
*Author—anonymous*

I make a conscious effort to live my life as many of the Top 5% live their lives:

Watch Your Thoughts
*Watch Your Thoughts.*
*They Become Words.*
*Watch your Words.*
*They Become Actions.*
*Watch Your Actions.*
*They Become Habits.*
*Watch Your Habits.*
*They Become Character.*
*Watch Your Character.*
*For It Becomes Your Destiny.*
*Author unknown*

Our daily actions create and break habits that control our lives. As I have previously mentioned, when we brush our teeth in the morning, we no longer think of the process anymore because we have done it enough times. The Top 5% control the habits they have in their life—always being aware of the bad ones as well as the good ones. As we discussed before, awareness precedes effective change—we cannot change anything in our lives if we are not aware of our present situation. We do not break old habits; we simply replace them with new ones. The first question is, are we aware of our bad habits? Once we are aware of our bad habits, then the second question is: how do we replace them with new and better habits?

In order to create a habit we need to perform that action for twenty-one days, every single day (15). If we stop for one day, we have to start over again. For instance, if we want to develop a habit of reading everyday, we need to read for twenty minutes everyday for the next twenty-one days. After that point it will be uncomfortable for an individual not to read twenty minutes a day.

Anthony Robbins once said, "There are two primary reasons why we will want to change anything in our lives. The first is "inspiration"(18); something inspires you enough to make a change in your life be it in your business, be it in your personal life, in the end my belief is our business and personal lives are interrelated.

There better be a good balance there, there better be happiness and there better be success on both sides. If not, it is going to weigh you down on both sides. Unfortunately, most people do not make drastic changes in their businesses and lives due to inspiration, because in order for you to get inspired, your mind has to be open to it, your parachute needs to be opened, and you have to chase inspiration.

The second reason why anyone would change anything in their life is desperation and pain.(18) When somebody sits there and says "I am getting frustrated with where I am," I say that is good, build on it, get it to a point where you are forced to make a change. We live in our comfort zones. We want different results each and every year, but we do not want to leave our comfort zones. We need to come to the realization and accept the fact that new development, growth and change can only effectively take place when it occurs outside of our comfort zones. What is it in your life that frustrates you? What is it that you have been complaining about? Why is it that we have been complaining and frustrated about the same thing for so long but have yet to make a change?

Imagine this . . . you are walking down the street and you see this cute dog, sitting on a porch, and as you are walking by he gets up like he is in some sort of pain, howls and sits back down again. What really gets your attention is the dog periodically keeps doing the same thing. Since we are creatures of curiosity, you walk up to the owner and you ask, "why is it that your dog howls as if it's in some sort of pain and then sits back down?"

"That's very simple, he's sitting on a nail."

"Alright, why doesn't he move?"

"You see that spot he is sitting has been his comfort zone for the last five years and now suddenly there is a nail there, but it doesn't hurt bad enough for him to move, to leave his comfort zone, to make a change."

How many of us actually have nails in our lives that we complain about on and off, for the last two or three years, but it just does not hurt bad enough to make that change that you are so intimately aware of. But it hurts bad enough to complain about it for the last three years and it changes how we think on a daily basis and affect us in more ways than we realize. Think about this for a second, how effective are we within the confines of our comfort zones? Are we able to attain all that we desire? What is your comfort zone? What opportunities are passing you by?

Earlier we talked about the freedom of choice . . . how we are entirely free to make our own decisions. Have we ever reached a point in which we have abused this privilege? We tend to have these habits of always changing strategies and it is usually done overnight! Over and over again we scratch good ideas for better ones without knowing when or how to begin implementation. The key is in knowing the starting point and the desired outcome. Until we know our starting and end points, we will never know if we are heading in the right direction. The danger of not knowing our direction is that it can lead us away from our path.

If you want to take your business, your relationships and your life to the next level, you have to be willing to get out of your comfort zone. As I mentioned previously, we are emotional creatures, so why do we go to our customers and try to convince them logically that they should do business with us? We have to touch their hearts, logic is not passion, it only takes one minute to affect change; it is a matter of one emotional decision. This decision is based upon us opening our minds and exiting our comfort zones. By doing this, the process of change has effectively begun.

*"How effective are we within the confines of our comfort zones?"*

# NOTES:
List 10 things you would like to change in your life.

# DNA of The Top 5%

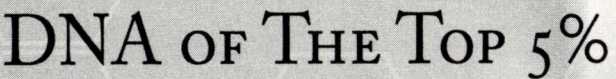

**2**

Link Choices to
Desired Outcome

DNA of the
Top 5%

# "If I Only Knew"
## Link Choices to Desired Outcome

*"Destiny is not a matter of chance, it is a matter of choice;
it is not a thing to be waited for, it is a thing to be achieved."*
*William Jennings Bryan*

The truth of the matter is what holds us back; it is not the circumstances that we find ourselves in; the economy is not to blame for our lack of satisfaction; nor are the people with whom we surround ourselves responsible for our sense of self-worth. The choices we make in our everyday lives dictate the burdens and blessings that we each encounter. The quality of our lives pivots on the quality of the choices that we make. A few bad decisions and life looks as if it is working against you. A few wise choices and like pieces to a well-designed puzzle, your future begins to take shape.

First we make our choices and then our choices make us. I believe life's formula is very simple. We are where we are today because of the choices we made last year. It is as simple as that. Really, the only question is, where do you want to be in one

year from now? How about two years from now? Where do
you want your business to be and are you planning on making
different decisions than you have made in the past? Where do
you want your relationships with your partner and/or children
to be?

Joe was a house builder and when the time came he approached his boss and said, "I'm retiring." His boss asked one
favour of Joe. He said "Joe you worked for me for a long time
and I know the quality of work that you do. I need one very
important house to be finished, could you finish that for me?"
Joe agreed. Knowing that this is the last home that he is going
to build before he retires, he does not use the best products
and does not use the best supplies. He does not create the best
quality construction, and does not create the best foundation.
When he finishes the home, he goes back to his boss and he
says "now I'm going to retire." And his boss turns to him and
says, "Joe you worked for me for many years, and you've been
very loyal to me, and for that loyalty you've just built your own
retirement home, a retirement gift from us to you."

What do you think Joe thought about at that point in
time? *If I only knew I was building my own retirement home I
would have made different choices.'* Life rarely makes mention to
you which decisions are going to be the important ones. There
are some more obvious events that will have significant impact
in our lives, but they are normally easily recognizable. We tend
to be on our best behaviour when making those decisions. The
truth of the matter is that everything we do, every single day,
at home and with our businesses, has profound effects on our
lives. Even with our customers, everything that we do, every
choice we make, leads to building our 'retirement home.' And
in turn, leads us to our ultimate purpose.

# IF I HAD THE PERFECT CIRCUMSTANCES
# LIFE WOULD BE EASIER . . .
# BUT I DON'T—NOW WHAT?

Our circumstances can help us create a history and a legacy to leave behind. A legacy that can change lives beyond our time. When we use the word "legacy," most people think of something large and tangible. Leaving behind a legacy does not have to be something tangible. The legacy that I would like to leave behind is a way of thinking that people will adapt and pass along after my time, *'a legacy of compassion.'* One of the most meaningful accomplishments is to open the minds and touch the hearts of others. That can be accomplish in one small moment of caring.

The most effective way of opening the minds of others is by understanding how you live your life on a daily basis, the decisions that you make when there seems to be no light in the end of the tunnel, as Washington Roebling lived his life.

The Brooklyn Bridge truly is a miraculous bridge. It spans the east river linking Manhattan to Brooklyn. In 1863, it became the vision of one man, a creative engineer named John Roebling. However, bridge building experts from all around the world, told him that it could not be done.

## *"The quality of our lives pivots on the quality of the choices we make."*

Roebling had a vision; he had set his sites on a goal to make it happen. He was determined to prove the skeptics wrong. He had a son named Washington, a young up-and-coming engineer, whom he convinced that this vision could become a reality. Together, they thought of ways to overcome the obstacles that stood ahead of them. As well, they developed concepts on how to take on such an overwhelming task. They harnessed their excitement and inspiration, to use as motivation to hire their crew to begin to build their dream bridge. Only a few months into the construction of the bridge, a tragic accident occurred, that would eventually take the life of John Roebling. Three years later, Washington was crippled when he developed caissons disease, or what is today known as the bends. Everyone felt as though the towel would have to be thrown in, seeing as how the Roebling's were in fact the only ones who believed that their bridge could be built.

> *"Life rarely makes mention to you which decisions are going to be the important ones."*

However, Washington was determined to finish the bridge and did so by way of telescope and by dictating orders to his wife from his bedroom window. The flame of desire to complete the bridge was only fueled by the death of his father. For at least ten years, he dictated instructions that his wife relayed to the engineers who in turn were able to complete the spectacular Brooklyn Bridge.(4)

> *"Our circumstances can help us create history and a legacy to leave behind. A legacy to change lives beyond our time."*

What circumstances are holding you back? What are you unnecessarily sacrificing because of the circumstances in your life? Your response will yield one of two results; it will either create history, a legacy or create regret.

One thing we have to understand is that no matter who we are, no matter what we do, and no matter what our background is, we all have our own unique set of circumstances. Since we cannot change that, we might as well start changing the way we think about them.

### *"We can only last for the long term if we tie what we need to do to purpose."*

If Washington can build a bridge from a bedroom window, what is it that we are able to build in our lives? Everything that we do should be tied to a purpose, as purpose is the greatest motivator.

As employers, your staff needs to be able to see the purpose of their tasks in order for them to go above and beyond for you. If there is no purpose, there is no need to sacrifice, and the easiest road will be taken. The easiest road has a high price; your dreams and your passions.

### *"Your response will yield one of two results; it will either create history or regret."*

Rick Allen, the drummer for Def Leopard, was involved in a severe car accident at the age of 21, on New Years Eve, 1984. Doctors re-attached his arm but when infection ensued they were forced to amputate (2). Now I am not much of a drummer, but I know that to be considered one of the world's best drummers you have to have both your arms. What would most people do in that situation? Most would give up and quit, quit on their dreams.

Rick had a critical decision to make. He could either follow the path of least resistance and let his circumstances control his life as well as take away his dreams, or he could take control of his circumstances and in turn, take control of his life. That decision would impact the rest of his life. Every single one of us hits that fork in the road at one point or another in our lives. One who chooses to take the road less traveled, will in turn, leave behind a legacy.

No matter what we do with the circumstances in our lives, there is always another circumstance or situation waiting for us. The question is how do we look at the circumstances we have? Rick Allen had the choice to give up, but the choice that he made was to recreate a whole new drum set and relearn how to drum with one arm and two legs.

*"The easiest road has a high price; your dreams and your passion."*

What circumstances do we have in our lives that stop us from doing what we know we need to do for our business and for our relationships to take them to the next level? What knowledge do we need to acquire and what actions need to be taken in order to overcome the obstacles that are before us. The only thing that stops us from taking it to the next level is the excuses that we convince ourselves with. These circumstances (excuses) are not always easy to overcome but it is the process of changing our way of thinking that will aid us in achieving our desired life.

What kind of circumstances do we have? I would like you to do something right now. Cross your arms, now cross them the other way. How comfortable is that? Is it as comfortable?

Not comfortable? A little bit harder? Now can you imagine all you have done all your life is to learn how to drum with two arms and two legs and all of a sudden have to re-teach yourself how to forget that habit and replace with one arm and two legs.

Think of the circumstances we have that are stopping us from expanding our business. What are the circumstances that hinder us in obtaining the visions, the forecasts, and the goals we had set? Our circumstances can help us create a personal history, a legacy to leave behind; a legacy to change lives beyond our time. Take a few moments to think about what circumstances are stopping you from achieving what you want out of life.

*"One who chooses the road less traveled in return will leave a legacy of their own."*

Leadership is not only about what we achieve in life, but how we live our life on a daily basis, how we think on a daily basis, what we think about, what we think about the people in our lives and what we think about the strangers that pass through our lives.

Which one are you?

Someone once shared a story with me about a girl who was struggling in life. She had complained to her father about how she felt that it was just too hard for her to overcome her problems. It seemed that just as she had a handle on one another problem would arise. She was tired of struggling. She did not know how she was going to make it, and simply wanted to give up.

Her father, who was a chef, took her into the kitchen,

without saying a word he grabbed three pots. Filled them with water and placed them upon the stove. Once the father had the three pots came to a boil, he placed carrots in one, eggs in another, and ground coffee beans in the third one. He just let them boil. The daughter who was growing increasingly impatient wondered what he was doing. After 20 minutes, he turned off the burners then fished out the carrots, placed them in a bowl, did the same for the eggs, placing them in a separate bowl. Then he ladled the coffee out and also placed it into a separate bowl. Turning to his daughter he said, "Darling, what do you see?"

"Carrots, eggs and coffee" she replied.

He brought her right up to the counter and asked her to feel the carrots. As she did, she recognized that they were soft. Then he asked her to break one of the eggs. She did, and after removing its shell she observed the hardboiled egg. Finally, he asked her to taste the coffee. After tasting the rich liquid, she smiled and humbly asked, "what does all this have to do with me?"

He turned to her and explained that each of these things had faced the same adversity—boiling water, yet each had a different reaction. The carrot, once strong and hard, became soft and weak. The fragile egg protected only by a thin outer shell, was hardened on the inside. The coffee beans however, were quite unique. After being placed in the boiling water, they changed the water itself. Then he asked "so which one are you?" "When adversity presents itself, how will you respond?" "Are you the carrot, the egg or the coffee bean?"

As a message to each of us, I think this story awakens us to the idea that the greatest part of our happiness or our misery solely depends on our reactions and not necessarily our circumstances.

*If I had perfect circumstances, life would be much easier, but I don't, so now what?* First and foremost, we need to recognize that there are no perfect circumstances, yet everyone has circumstances that may or may not hold them back. We have to make the conscious decision to control them rather than allow them to have control of us. For by doing so, they cannot keep us held back.

Our history, our legacy depends on our control of these circumstances. This is what the great leaders do. They take control of their circumstances by changing their state of mind and use them to their advantage. Thus allowing them to grow, learn, and better themselves.

It is merely our way of thinking that blocks us from attaining a life that we know we truly deserve. Everything we do on a daily basis is a result of planting seeds for the long term. We will reap the rewards of the seeds we plant. When we plant dandelions seeds we get dandelions, when we plant apple seeds we get apples.

> **"We have to be willing to give up immediate satisfaction in order to have a larger, delayed gratification."**

If you have ever painted the interior of a house before, was the process longer to put a primer on than it did to just apply the actual paint colour? Those who never have used a primer probably view it as being a waste of time. It seems, in the beginning, like a waste of time. Why paint the walls with primer when you are just going to repaint over again. For the long term is it more effective to use a primer? Absolutely. I remember when I had painted a wall in my house red as the focal point of the living room. Because it was a dark color and I was painting over a light beige color I did not bother taking the time to prime the wall, at that moment it seemed like a waste of time. It took me 4–5 coats of paint in order to finish that wall. In hindsight, if I had put one coat of primer, I would have finished that wall with a maximum of two coats and probably with better quality. Not to mention it would have lasted longer, saving me both time and money. This goes the same for businesses and personal relationships.

We need to start thinking about the long term when we are building our lives, when we are building our relationships—business and personal. Are we chasing the next deal, or are we planting seeds for the next year?

In order to increase our financial worth—when we look at investments, in order to make more money we must be willing to give up money in the beginning for investing. Invest a little money now so it can grow in the future. It is the same when it comes to the choices we make about our businesses, lives and time—we have to be willing to give up immediate satisfaction in order to have a larger, delayed gratification.

Most people would say that Albert Einstein was a genius, and what made him a genius was that his way of thinking was so simple and basic. As he said "The problems we face today cannot be solved with the same level of thinking that created them." It is a very simple concept really, if we want to achieve different results we must take a different approach. If you want to obtain the success or the levels of relationships that the great leaders have, then you must do as they have done, which is apply the 7 Principles into every aspect of your life. Make life very simple; make your business very simple.

First we make our choices; then our choices make us.

Can you imagine not having any choices? The power of choice is truly the greatest gift bestowed upon us, yet so many of us take this power for granted. Choices promote change and change provides growth. By taking this gift for granted we are halting our personal and professional growth. The wrong choices are always the easiest to make, it is the right ones that prove to be difficult. Where would you be today if you had made the right choices five years ago? If you did, congratulations! Now let me ask you this, where do you think you will be in the next five years if you make all the right choices? As I had mentioned choice is our greatest gift—not one to be taken for granted or to be neglected.

*Life is about who you love and who you hurt.*
*It's about who you make happy or unhappy purposefully.*
*It's about keeping or betraying trust.*
*It's about friendship, used as a sanctity or a weapon.*
*It's about what you say and mean,*
*maybe hurtful, maybe heartening.*
*About starting rumors and contributing to petty gossip.*
*It's about what judgments you pass and why.*
*And who your judgments are spread to.*
*It's about who you've ignored with full control and intention.*
*It's about jealousy, fear, ignorance, and revenge.*
*It's about carrying inner hate and love,*
*letting it grow, and spreading it.*
*But most of all, it's about using your life to touch or poison other*
*people's hearts in such a way that could have never occurred alone.*
*Only you choose the way those hearts are affected,*
*And those choices are what life's all about.*
*- Author unknown -*

# NOTES:
List the choices that you know deep within you need to be made.

# DNA of The Top 5%

DNA of the
Top 5%

**3**
Keep your
commitments

# "WILL YOU MARRY ME?"
## KEEP YOUR COMMITMENTS

*"If we do not discipline ourselves the world will do it for us."*
*William Feather*

Commitment will make you stronger. Commitment will make you highly desirable. Commitment will make you more sensitive. Commitment will make you among the elite in the world. Commitment will make you smile. Commitment will make you much more productive.

What do you think about when we talk about commitment? Do the same thoughts that you have go through the minds of those around you? Does the thought of commitment make you feel anything? What goes through your heart when you think of commitment?

Take for example, a case of two distinctly different people. The first appears to have superior abilities, talent, and education, yet, is unable to produce the quality of life that he or she thinks that they want. The second, having a considerable number of disadvantages, is not described as being naturally talented or 'blessed' with abilities yet they manage to create the quality of life that they want.

The difference in the quality of life has nothing to do with capabilities or the advantages that you may have been born with. Take Oprah Winfrey for example, she was born and raised extremely poor . . . so poor in fact that she refers to it as "po," for she says that they could not even afford the "or." Yet she overcame her circumstances, and created her own empire.

### *"Commitment will make you among the elite in the world."*

She never lost touch with who she really is. By keeping herself humbled she has impacted so many lives through her Angel Network Foundation and the many other charities that she has formed and supported over the years. She realizes her fortune and feels the need to give back. She never once lost focus because she was more then committed to attaining all that she knew she deserved.

When you do what is right, even if it costs you in the short term, it will always pay off in the long run. In the course of human history, I wonder how many people fell short of accomplishing a goal when the light at the end of the tunnel was in sight. You are either going to choose to be different or you are going to be the same. It is always easier to blame someone or to blame something else than to look in the mirror.

Let's have a look at the most common depiction of commitment. You are about to get married and find yourself walking down the isle. Okay as a side note, I am going to pick on the men here because I have learned better than to pick on women. It is time to exchange the vows and your wife-to-be has finished proclaiming her undying and unparalleled love for you. Now it is your turn . . .

You start by talking about the life you are both going to build together and the dreams that you have for your future. Not the ones that you are simply going to chase, but the real ones, the ones that you know you are destined to accomplish. Confidently you state, "I am one-hundred percent committed and loyal to you for the rest of my life." Then you stop. Taking a step back, with a slight squint in your eyes you clear your throat and say, "Actually, what I mean is that I'll be ninety-nine point nine percent committed and loyal to you. You see, I want to put that point one percent in my pocket just in case."

How do you think the bride is going to think, and more importantly feel, at that moment? Embarrassed? Confused? Betrayed? Imagine what she is feeling? Hurt, no doubt. Perhaps even feelings of stupidity flood over her for having let you into her life to begin with.

In business is 99.9% commitment enough for you? Let's face it, 99.9% is a value so close to 100% that we feel compelled to accept it. Why then would it be a problem for a bride to have to accept it on one of the most precious days of her life? Would it have mattered if you said 2% or 99%? Truthfully, no, it would not have made an iota of difference. In the simple example outlined here, we can see that both the bride and groom need to be unified on their interpretation of commitment. It is not unreasonable of the bride (or anyone for that matter) to expect 100% commitment in a relationship. Admission of withholding loyalty is an affirmation that the commitment is not complete. Commitment starts no less than 100%.

How committed are we when we make our forecasts? When we make our goals what level of commitment are we expecting to put into them? When we start to action our visions where do we really stand? Doing things for your customers, for your co-workers, and for your loved ones, requires the true commitment that you know they are counting on.

Certainly you will not be surprised when you start to realize how most people treat their customers and acquaintances in business with more respect than their own family, when it comes to day-to-day commitments. Do we sit there and say I am 100% committed to you as long as it is convenient to me? A lot of people break those small little promises; small lies, and white lies, as they call them. If you break enough white lies you will start to lose the ability to distinguish them from all the other colours of mistruths and lies.

Commitment starts no lower than 100%. Commitment does not mean as long as it is convenient. Making a commitment is a way of thinking. If you break your commitment, even to yourself, then people will trust your words less. You must be diligent in sticking to your commitments. Let your yes be your yes, and your no be your no. If people sense that you are not serious about your life, then why should they feel compelled to help you along the path of success?

A short while ago, there was a new 'phenom' on the market: his name; Tiger Woods. People still love to watch him play; he did for golf what Subaru did for the World Rally Circuit. He outperformed the competition and made the game exciting to watch. He performs his required tasks with such dedication and ease that it is almost unfathomable that the records he has broken have stood as long as they have.

People sit there and look at Tiger Woods and wonder, what makes him break records? Tiger Woods first picked up a golf club at the age of two years. Believe it or not it, it was during his earliest years that he realized that he had a passion for this sport. As he got older, he committed himself everyday to master the game, and follow in the steps of his mentors, to become one of the world's best. It is due to his everyday commitment that got him where he is, but more importantly, it is this commitment that keeps him there.

> *"The wrong choices are always the easiest to make, it is the right ones that prove to be difficult."*

As a woman, what is the first thing that comes to mind when your partner comes home with a dozen long stem roses? Is your response along the lines of, "what did you do?," "what do you want?," or "no, you are not going golfing on Sunday?"

Which is more valuable to you as an individual? Those types of grand gestures that may sometimes be few and far between, or the little things that he / she may do for you on a more regular basis? Obviously, it is the little things. Commitment is those little things that we do on a consistent basis. It is the foundation for how we think and how we live our lives. Now if you were to do more of the little things daily for your partner, think about how much more valuable those grand gestures then become.

Go back to the little things when dealing with your customers and relationships in life. How excited do you get when you know you are lined up to achieve a big result, or navigated successfully, and are ready to land a big deal? Conversely, how excited are we to work with customers for something small, something where we may not see an actual result until further down the road?

Early French-Canadian lumberjacks understood that

there was nothing magical about the final swing of l'hache even though it is the one that finally fells the tree. It is the incremental work that we put into things that accomplishes our goals. The manner through which we observe and react to our lives, reveals just what progressive steps need to be taken in order to accomplish our goals.

If you have not guessed it already, I hope it does not come as a surprise. When things do not seem to be changing the way we think they should, it is time to change the way we think. What few people recognize is the level of commitment Tiger Woods has sustained since he was two years old. The result of that commitment is what we delight in when we watch him play.

A humorous anecdote: Some farm animals decided that they wanted to surprise their farmer with a great breakfast. The next morning, on her breakfast table, the farmer found wonderfully prepared bacon and eggs with fresh milk. In this story the chicken and cow were involved but the pig was committed.

Are you committed to your vision, goals and dreams or are you just planning on being involved? How committed are you to bettering your life?

*"Commitment is those little things that we do on a consistent basis. It is the foundation for how we think andhow we live our lives."*

Indifference is a feeling of apathy. If indifference is not the proper way to describe your general feeling about life, then perhaps committed is. Commitment is your foundation. If you are not 100% committed to what it is that you are working towards, your efforts will be futile. Commitment is the fundamental step towards achieving your desired outcome. How committed are you to your future successes?

# NOTES:
List the commitments you are going to make daily,
weekly, and monthly.

# DNA of The Top 5%

DNA of the
Top 5%

**4**
Be Willing
To Fail

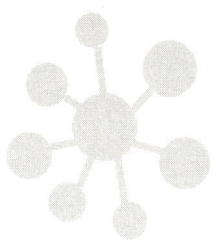

# What If I Were To Fail?
## Be Willing to Fail

*"The way to succeed is to double your failure rate."*
*Thomas Watson*

Usually, most would want to refine and correct their practices until they become absolutely perfect, because of their fear of failure. The problem they find is that they spend so much time trying to accomplish one single task that a majority of their other potential wins have passed them by.

Children, when asked to describe what darkness is, will often borrow the notion that darkness is merely the absence of light. In effect, they are suggesting that darkness, in itself, does not exist. How then can we as adults apply that to failure? You have probably already drawn the parallels. We need to better condition ourselves to understand that failure is not something to fear.

*Be willing to fail.*

An infant is learning to walk and he is having a very difficult time at it. "Why can't I get this right?" he thinks to himself. Frustration starts to set in and eventually he just goes back to crawling. Seeing his frustration and appreciating how difficult it really must be to learn to walk for the first time, do you let him crawl the rest of his life? "Don't bother trying to walk anymore, little baby boy. It's not worth the trouble." These are hardly the words we would expect any parent to say. In fact, we encourage them to keep at it until they are finally able to function under their own power. What is it about their will that allows them to continually try and try? When in our lives did we lose that desire that we innately possess? When did we become stagnant? At what point in your life did you feel it was okay to just exist and no longer pursue your desires? It is often said that any dead fish can float downstream. In order to swim with the great leaders, do not be the 95% that follow the path of least resistance. You must be willing to fail in order to be a part of the top 5%, those who swim against the current.

Failures are a part of life. Will we solve them or complain about them? Be thankful for your adversities. Adversity is what makes us who we are, it is our strength, it is our guidance, and it is part of our character. Do not use your adversities as a crutch and a reason to feel sorry for yourself.

> ### *"Fire is the test for gold;*
> ### *Adversity, of strong men."*

Most people have a fear. It may be a fear of heights or a fear of snakes. Others may not have such a tangible fear; they have a fear of failure or success. To some degree, we all do because we are all human beings. Fear is an emotion that we all feel yet not all emotions are real. They are only real to us because we have convinced ourselves of them.

F—False

E—Evidence

A—Appearing

R—Real

*Neale Donald Walsche*

Fear and faith are both false emotions that we have grown to believe. Our beliefs are a direct reflection of our outcome. Neither fear nor faith are real, they are both false emotions. It is up to us, which we chose as our belief system.

How grand would it be, to climb a mountain and stand a top its summit? Although, it could be an experience of a lifetime, the majority of people, would more then likely shy away due to the element of danger and the fear of falling. What if there was absolutely zero percent chance of failure? I think if this was the case, then more people would be willing to make the attempt to experience the views from the peak and revel in their sense of accomplishment. Along the same lines it is time to pose a question to you:

What kind of decisions, commitments and choices would you have made in the past if you knew you could not fail? Where would you be and what would you have achieved?

Now if you were able to make choices without any fear of the outcome . . . where do you think this mentality would take you in the future?

Who is this person?

AGE

23 Ran for Legislature—failed

24 Failed in business

26 Sweetheart died

27 Had a nervous breakdown

29 Defeated for Speaker

34 Defeated for Congress

37 Elected to Congress

39 Defeated for Congress

45 Defeated for Senate

46 Defeated for nomination for Vice President

49 Defeated for Senate

51 Elected President of the United States

Answer: Abraham Lincoln (1). Almost every year of his life seemingly resulted in failure. It took me a very long time to understand the true relevance of this. You see, this was my missing piece out of my puzzle, the missing piece that the great leaders carried around with them. One of the most powerful lines you can walk away with, *'if you want to succeed in anything you endower in life you have to be willing to fail at it first.'*

You cannot succeed without failing. Books on leadership have been written about Abraham Lincoln, and seemingly his life was full of failure. It was this failure that granted him his greatest successes.

We are conditioned from the time we are children that failing is bad, and as soon as we have learned to link failure to something negative we will spend the rest of our lives avoiding failure. That is why 95% of the people out there avoid failure; unfortunately success is always on the other side of failure.

It is not like the Top 5% does not have a fear of failure; we all have them, the only difference is that they are willing to do the things that 95% of the people are not willing to do in order to get in life what the 95% of the people will never achieve. The only way you have failed is if you are not willing to make another attempt towards success.

Did you know that Walt Disney went bankrupt several times and Henry Ford five times before they succeeded?(9)

In the Baseball Hall of Fame as a hitter, to be the world's best . . . to be the best of the best, you only have to succeed 30% of the time on average and fail approximately 70% of the time.

When you see the best in your industry, go up to them and ask them one question, "How many times have they put themselves in a position to fail and also how many of those times did they actually fail as well in their life?"

Sylvester Stallone, best known for his portrayal of Rocky Balboa, had the vision to create the movie 'Rocky.' The problem was he had a hard time selling his vision. No one else saw the end product the way that he did.

How many times do we have a vision of where we want to take our business, and where we want to take our life, but nobody wants to buy into our vision and so we give up easily? We have this great vision, we get so excited, and then we talk to the first person and they say, "it would never work, why would you want to do that?" "Yeah you're right," and that is where it ends, we give up. Every individual will go through his or her life at one point or another, carrying with them a faded vision. A vision of what they want to create, a vision of what legacy they want to leave behind, and a vision of the life that they want to live.

The difference with the Top 5% is that they know that it is their vision to see and not the responsibility of others and believe wholeheartedly in it. It is their vision, and therefore only they are accountable to follow through with it to the end. Sylvester Stallone went to almost 200 producers with that script and everybody said it would never work but he was committed, not only when it was convenient, he was committed to the end. After awhile, he ran out of money, and he was living in his car while he was trying to sell that script. But he would not give up. Finally, with only one hundred and six dollars left in his pocket and living out of his car, a producer offered him approximately twenty thousand dollars for that script. That was an incredible amount of money. But the deal was he was not going to star in the movie. But you see he was committed to his vision to the end, so he said no. They proceeded to offer him eighty, then one hundred thousand dollars, and then finally three hundred thousand dollars, but Stallone refused to sell the script unless he was the lead. In the end, he sold the script for the original twenty thousand dollars with him playing the lead. To this day, the Rocky series has grossed over one billion dollars in revenue and has made Stallone a household name. (12) He kept going until somebody finally said, "We'll take a chance on you." And many sequels later, most people sit there and say, he got so lucky with that movie, that movie made him big. People are right; that movie did make him, but what they do not understand is he created his own luck.

*"The difference with the Top 5% is that they know it is their vision and not others to see and believe. It is their vision and therefore only they are accountable to follow through with it to the end."*

Success is on the other side of failure. To succeed at anything, we have to be willing to fail first. Neither success nor failure is an overnight experience; each consists of the sum of our daily activities. Success or failure is cumulative over a week . . . a month . . . a year . . . a lifetime.

Success is based on a way of thinking, a philosophy of life. When most people think of success or failure, they think of these giant things. Failure is the result of not following through, not making that call, not reading that book, not taking the time with your kids, not saying I love you, not giving 100%—that creates ultimate failure in life.

Success is taking one step at a time. It is just like building a brick wall; you must lay each brick individually, in order to successfully build a wall that will last a lifetime. It is successfully doing what it takes, making the call, and following through, that allows you to build a foundation that will stand the test of time, much like that of a brick wall.

In the beginning, if you try to lift a heavy weight you will fail. It is going to seem impossible, never to be able to succeed. Why bother trying? If you approach it little by little, and increase the weight as time goes on, you will be able to lift that weight. That is the same as fear. Approach it a step at a time, little by little.

If you take a risk, you might still fail, if you do not risk, you have already failed. The greatest risk is to do nothing and seemingly exist in the path of life.

Take risks, be daring. Be willing to fail.

*"Success is going from one failure to another*
*without the loss of enthusiasm"*
*Winston Churchill*

**NOTES:**
What are your greatest fears?

**NOTES:**
If you could make choices without any fear of failure,
what choices would you make?

# DNA OF THE TOP 5%

DNA of the
Top 5%

**5**
Focus On
Your Goals

# I Have Gained Success But Not Happiness
## Focus on Your Goals

*"Obstacles are those frightful things you see when you take your eyes off your goal."*
*Hannah More 1745–1833 British Reformer & Philanthropist*

The day I heard Herman Cane speak at a conference changed my perception of success. Cane came from a family with very little, his father worked three jobs in order to give his family a chance at the success they deserved. Herman Cane worked his way up the ladder against all odds, in order to reach his dreams. After years of commitment to his goal, he had arrived to what he believed to be considered success, the golden office of an executive with Burger King. Sitting in his new office, he realized that even though he had become successful, he was not happy. It is that day I realized my perception of success misleading. Success in not the position that you attain, it is the way of thinking at any level of your life, which will grant you success, and in turn give you happiness.

We need to understand that life is about how we think and about how we respond to our given circumstances. A level of balance and consistency needs to be present in the way we think and work at home. We can gain all the financial success and reach our desired corporate positions, but still have incorrect thinking patterns. If we do not have the right way of thinking in our lives on a daily basis, we will always be chasing blind success with the blurred perception that we are actually chasing happiness.

To be happier at work, we need to be happier in our lives. We must realize that chasing a goal will never lead us to satisfaction, but chasing a purpose will give us meaning in our lives, and a sense of fulfillment.

One thing that I have noticed, in working with thousands of individuals from all walks of life, is that everything that you do leads you down one path or another. You might be thinking that this is being overly simplified; yet you realize that it really is just that simple. The path of happiness and success in your endeavors is the one that we typically seek. The path of regret, pain, and imbalance in your life is the one we want to shun.

Everything that we do in life, on a daily basis, is planting these seeds for the long term. Every seed that you plant should head you towards a destination where you can create a balance in your life, a balance with work and personal life.

* * *

Being a Boy Scout really exposed me to covert 'life-lessons' most of which, I am sure, have passed me by. One such lesson that I did manage to grasp, was during a simple contest that we were having during one of our frequent winter camps at Algonquin Park in Northern Ontario. The task was simple;

walk the straightest possible line across a field of freshly fallen snow. Now I will be the first to admit that although we were a great group of friends, we really were not very imaginative in our challenges when we were young.

So how would you approach this simple task? What procedures would you employ to help ensure that the line that you are going to walk is not just straighter than the other competitor, but the straightest line possible?

In order to attain the success we desire, it is important to learn to focus on our goals. Our daily activities should revolve around accomplishing our longer-term goals.

Staying focused on your feet, carefully placing one foot in front of the other, would allow you to monitor and maintain correctness in each and every step that you take. However, we need to be wary of ever-slight deviations from the goal. What if with every second step we were one degree off? If we were looking down all the time, we probably would not realize until we had become significantly off course. Where do you think we would have ended up after two hundred yards? Way off course!

Selecting a prominent landmark in the distance provides you with a means by which you can measure your progress. By remaining fixed on your goals, in my case a large pine, staying on track is infinitely easier than micro-managing each and every step.

**"Shortsightedness often leads us into the nearest wall."**

If you do not know where you want to end up, your greatest opportunities could pass right by you while you are traveling in the opposite direction.

There are many times when I have driven down the highway late at night and have witnessed cars that have hit an isolated lamp pole. Someone is driving down the street, there is barely any traffic on the road, and for whatever reason they lose control of their car and hit the only lamp-post to be found! What is that? Do lamp-posts have a magnetic pull that latches onto unsuspecting cars as they approach? The truth of the matter is that a driver tends to end up positioning the car in the direction they are looking.

It is equally true in golf that you are destined to hit the ball where you focus your concentration. If you approach a hole which has a precariously placed water hazard in front of the green, and your mindset shifts towards that of not hitting the ball in the water, you will likely end up doing just that. By focusing on the water, and not the green, your subconscious tells your body to hit the ball towards the water.

Focusing your energy towards the hazard will definitely result in you ending up there, but what about if you do actually want to hit the object of your focus? Would it then be better to remain fixed on the path the object is going to take? How about remaining fixated on the object itself?

Skeet shooting is not about aiming at the clay disc. Instead, it is about aiming to where the disc is going to be once the shotgun pellets have been discharged.

Would you agree that life is very much the same way? What is it that you are looking at? What is your vision? Do your everyday thought processes account for your growth and change? Focusing on your goals is important because ultimately, that is where you are going to end up.

Inevitably we are prone to losing sight of even the simplest things that we have been taught. I learned that lesson the hard way. I remember lying there on the ground, squinting into a blazing sun that was doing nothing but making an already uncomfortable situation more so. My ankle felt like it was shattered in a dozen pieces, I could barely breathe; the bruises on my ribs must have been visible through my leather jacket, because they hurt so much. One shoulder felt like a Mack truck hit it and the other one just felt as though it was gone. Even though the ambulance was there in a matter of minutes it could very well have been days. The pain was nothing shy of excruciating.

Flopping my head to one side, I peer at my track bike. It has to be in ten different pieces, four of which I did not even think possible! I had to have asked myself "if there was no one else around, how on earth did I run my motorcycle off the race track?" At the moment, I just could not understand what went wrong.

I was coming around the fastest turn on the racetrack and for a fleeting moment I felt fear. Not a great thing to have happen just before diving into a corner. The fear as slight and seemingly insignificant as it was, managed to take my focus from where I wanted it, and shifted it to what could go wrong.

I focused on the barricades on the side of the racetrack as I started thinking to myself, "what if I cannot make this corner at this speed, I will run right off the track." Then I remained fixated on the spot where I was destined to make impact. Keep one thing in mind, this whole process lasted no more than one to two seconds.

As with the Roger Banister example, our thoughts will always create our reality, and that is exactly what happened to me. You will always end up where you choose to remain fixated. At the speed of life, you had better ensure your eyes do not leave your visual mark of where you intend to end up.

Life goes very fast. You rarely have time to think, while going 200 km/h. If you look the wrong way you are ruined. That is the same thing with your business, personal relationships, and all aspects of your life. If you are not focusing, if you are not fixating every single second on where you want to end up, in a split second you could lose everything. You could lose your momentum.

What are you fixating on every single day? Are you letting the circumstances take over your life? Or are you controlling your circumstances and using them to your advantage? If you want something different *in* your life you have to be willing to do something different *with* your life.

> **"You will always end up where you choose to remain fixated."**

If it were easy, everyone would create happiness. No one ever said it would be easy, but it definitely can be simple. I have a dear friend of mine, and he has the most incredible talent, but he just cannot seem to get past this stage of stagnation in his life. Every year, and sometimes it seems like almost every month, he makes a list of goals and these resolutions. I know what he can do, and it is not even much of a stretch for him, but they are above and beyond what is considered average because of his talents. But after three weeks, circumstances kick into his life, again. He keeps letting the circumstances control him instead of taking control of the circumstances. Realizing that they will always be there no matter what he does, he wants different results. Every single year he makes his attempts, but he is not willing to do anything different. That is why he has been stuck for the last three years and no one can help him out of that except himself. Realizing this, he has begun to approach this differently. He has actually started setting goals and committed himself to them and in turn, is beginning to see the positive results from the choices and commitments he has made.

Learn to focus on your goals. Your daily activities should revolve around accomplishing your long-term goals. Short-sightedness often leads us to the nearest wall.

The reason why so many people have a hard time making choices is that they do not visualize their goal. If you can see your destination, when you then approach a fork in the road, the decision is simple. Choose the path that leads to your goal. However, prepare yourself because in most cases, it will not be the path of least resistance. Ask yourself, "What do I ultimately want out of this situation?" If you do not know where you want to end up, your greatest opportunities could pass right by you.

Goals will help you determine where it is that you want to end up. They are your road map. They will aid you in measuring your success and keep you focused. Once you have reached or surpassed your goals, there will come a great feeling of accomplishment. Never lose sight of striving to obtain that feeling.

*"Chasing a purpose will give us meaning in our lives, a sense of fulfillment."*

## NOTES:
How would you describe happiness?

## NOTES:
What goals will lead to your happiness in the long and short term?

# DNA of The Top 5%

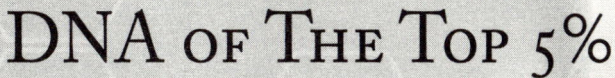

DNA of the
Top 5%

**6**

Be Aware of
Your Perceptions

# A Nine Year Old Boy
# Lost His Arm
## Be Aware of Your Perceptions

*"People are as happy as they make up their minds to be."*
*Abraham Lincoln*

Take a couple of seconds and ask yourself what emotions and feelings are going through your mind at this moment? Confusion? Excitement? Hot? Cold? Hunger? Keep that thought and imagine this; there is one way out of the room you are in at the moment. That door opens, and an angry, wild bear walks in, what are you going to be feeling now? Scared? What happened to hot, cold or excited? Are they gone? Just like that? Taking a second look, you realize that it is just your friend in a costume. In five seconds your perception changed three times, so your expectations changed three times, therefore your thought process has changed three times, all because of the changes to your emotional state. These perceptions even change our physiology, the chemistry in our body i.e. sweaty palms, faster heart beats etc . . .

In a fraction of a second, our perception can change our state of mind. Could we agree that every little thing we do with our customers and relationships changes perceptions? The things we do either change their perception of who we are and the industry, or reconfirms what they already knew. How we answer the phone, how we hang up the phone, what information we choose to send and what we talk about. All of these contribute to the perceptions that exist around us. Believe me when I insist that their perceptions will control their expectations. We control people's expectations of us by what we do on a daily basis including the choices and commitments that we make.

I was getting to the point of complete frustration when I had let my circumstances get the better of me. I remember dialing the phone as I thought to myself, "I feel sorry for the individual that answers," because I had decided not to have any mercy on them, I was going to let them have a piece of my mind.

I was in the midst of going through one of those phone bill issues that we all have had the misfortune of going through. My call was received and words could barely describe what ensued. Almost completely unbeknownst to be, my perceptions changed. The customer service representative that answered the phone knew what she was up against. Her mixture of voice, manners and concern really helped me believe that she wanted to help. In almost an instant my perception changed, and how I reacted changed dramatically. Remember, it is the everyday little things that often carry the most impact. Business is not about the big things that you do, it is about the little things that you do every single day consistently. That is commitment.

Perception changes the way you think and, in turn, the actions you will perform, leading to the outcome that you have. During a trip to Brazil, a friend and I were walking along a stretch of sandy beach. There was a small puddle about a decimeter in diameter, right in the middle of the beach, and it was bubbling through. I was examining it and surmised to my walking partner there was a perfectly natural ecological reason why it was happening in the middle of a beach in Rio.

> *"I was getting to the point of complete frustration when*
> *I had let my circumstances get the better of me."*

Granted, he had his own theory on the situation but I personally think my reason made more sense. Content that we had discovered the solution, we continued on our way. Surprisingly enough, we encountered another similar puddle. We looked at that puddle for a couple of minutes. A twelve year old boy happened by, so we called him over and tried to communicate with him. "Does this happen often?" I asked inquisitively, "what is it?" He doesn't say a word. Instead, He stoops over, swipes the sand 3 times and reveals the solution to our little mystery, a black plastic disc. Not a natural ecological phenomenon at all. It was a sprinkler head. Defeated, we looked at each other, shrugged our shoulders and walked away.

Our perception was that it was a natural, ecological phenomenon, so we had these great reasons; we talked about it and came up with a conclusion, a belief we would have lived with as a result of our perception. Our perceptions control everything we choose to believe. Our customers' perceptions control everything they choose to believe. Right now, your customers have a perception. Awareness precedes change—figure out what that perception is right now, before you try to change it. It is imperative to understand what it is you are trying to change.

As we mentioned earlier, if you walk in trying to talk to your kids with logic right away, you are wasting your time and will be frustrated in the process. Is that what you are doing with your customers? Do you walk in and try to sell to them based on logic, telling them why they should do business with us? At that point in time their minds are shut, you are wasting your time, you are wasting their time and you are frustrating them. Logic does not sell. Make sure that you take the time to deal with people in your lives with a balance of emotion and logic.

> *"Our perceptions control everything we choose to believe.*
> *Our customer's perceptions control everything*
> *they choose to believe."*

An interesting story, which was shared with me at a conference, can shed some light to how circumstances can be looked upon in several different ways. Mark White, Democrat (b.1940) was the forty-third governor of Texas. Every Sunday, he and his wife would take a drive down the country road. And one day when they were driving down, he pulled up into a gas station. As soon as he pulled up into the gas station, he noticed his wife's body language get very quiet. He did not say anything, the gas attendant came and filled up gas, and they drove off. A couple minutes later he looked at his wife and said, "Obviously something went through your mind, would you like to talk about it?" And she said "well, nothing major, just the gas attendant used to be my boyfriend in high school, and at that point in time I thought I was going to marry him."

So the governor looked at her and said "well good thing you didn't, because you'd be the wife of a gas attendant." And she looked at him, and said, "No, if I married him, the gas attendant would have been the governor."

We all have the ability to look at any situation or circumstance from various angles, and doing so, we control the lens through which we perceive our surroundings. The way in which any given situation or moment is viewed, is on account of the clarity of the lens that we are peering through. "To her lover a beautiful woman is a delight; to a monk she's a distraction; to a mosquito, a good meal." Perception is everything. (21)

A nine-year-old boy got into a car accident, and when he awoke he realized that he had lost his left arm. His parents tried to put him into different sports and events to build his self esteem. One of the things they put him into was Judo. The instructor in Judo is called 'Sensei.' For a couple of months, Sensei kept teaching the nine-year-old boy one move and one move only. After a couple of months the boy went up to his Sensei and asked "Isn't it time to learn a different move?"

To which Sensei replied, "No, you're not yet ready, you need to keep practicing that move before you move on."

After another couple of months had gone by, still only with that one move, the Sensei put the boy into competition. So he went and to his surprise, he started winning the matches. The competition came to a point where he was going to go on the mat for a bronze medal and to his surprise he won it with ease. The challenge for silver proved to be hardly any more difficult. When he got to the gold medal match he walks onto the mat, his opponent walks onto the mat—twice his size, twice as strong, both arms, twice the experience, twice the speed. Things looked grim, to the point where the referee even came up and told the Sansei, "Maybe we should call this off." To which the Sensei replied, "No, let him try."

How often do we step up to something that we want to accomplish in our lives and all of the sudden our competition who is twice our size comes up, and we just walk away, thinking why even bother?

> *"When we focus our energy on the negative, we consequently plant the seeds of negativity in our lives."*

That match went back and forth, back and forth, until his opponent grew frustrated and made a mistake, and that is when the boy used his one move. He won the match with that one move. On his way home he looked at his Sensei, and inquired, "Not that I'm complaining, but how was I able to win the gold medal being the smallest, the slowest, the least experience, with one arm and only one move?" "That's very simple to answer" His Sensei started, "first of all you've almost perfected the hardest move in judo, secondly the only counter to that move, is for your opponent to grab your left arm."

How do we look at our circumstances? Are our circumstances weaknesses or strengths? When most people would have taken his circumstance and equated it to his biggest weakness, his Sensei guided him on how to take it, and turn it into his biggest strength. How often do we give up easily based on the circumstances that we have and how we look at them? Let's be realistic, no matter what we do, no matter how much money we make, no matter where we live or who we know, we will always have circumstances. We cannot get rid of those. A mere shift in perception is enough to change your state of mind. We can control the power of our minds. When we focus our energy on the negative, we consequently plant the seeds of negativity in our lives.

If you focus more of your life around positive perceptions, the choices you make will lead to desirable outcomes. Is your glass half full or half empty?

*"Insanity is doing the same thing over and over again and expecting a different result."*
*Albert Einstein*

# NOTES:
List 5 perceptions that control your life.

# DNA of The Top 5%

**7**
Invest In Yourself

DNA of the Top 5%

# I Will Not Shower For Three Days
## Invest in Yourself

*"Great Leaders are in the business of learning"*

Great leaders are in the business of learning. They are always re-educating themselves; reading and stretching their minds each and every day. There is a lesson to be learned from this. What contributions do you make to your own growth? If the effort you are putting in is average, or less than average, then you should be completely prepared to accept the results of those investments. If, however, you are investing more than the average person, then you should be prepared for more than average results.

The average person reads only one book a year on instilling passion, desire and purpose to expand and grow their mind. These are not necessarily the people who have difficulty reading. These are the people who realize that learning is an investment. But what a pathetic investment we are all making. Only one book a year! If my math has not completely failed me that means in five years I can expect to have read only five books! Barely what even the 'average' person would consider investing in themselves, yet it is what we are doing.

What would happen if we would not have a shower for three days—how effective would we be? Would others want to deal with us? We take a shower everyday because we live in a dirty environment. Do we not live in a negative environment as well? No matter where we are, is it not true that there is someone complaining about one thing or another? How many of us get excited about working with someone that is negative? Just as we take twenty minutes out of our morning to shower and clean our bodies, should we not also take twenty minutes everyday to clean our minds?

### *"Realize that learning is an investment."*

How would twenty minutes of reading a day contribute towards your investment in yourself? Ten minutes over breakfast, or at your desk before checking your e-mails, and perhaps ten minutes during lunch, or on break, or even before retiring for the night. Imagine if you committed yourself to reading just twenty minutes a day, perhaps ten pages. In one month one could easily read a book. It does not have to be a big book; just something that you feel will be an investment in your growth. Something you feel will be a quality piece of writing, which will bring quality ideas and thoughts to your mind. Words that will have you continually thinking. In five short years you could read somewhere in the neighborhood of sixty books. Compare that with the 'average' five books in five years and guess where you find yourself; in the Top 5%.

With that type of investment, where could you be in five

years within your industry? You would be well on your way to joining the Top 5%. I say this because the amount of information that you would have been able to accumulate is easily ten fold greater than the 'average' person around you and now all you have to do is commit to the information.

We are where we are today because of the books we have read and the people we have associated with for the last five years. If you want a clearer picture of where your business is going to be in the next five years, all you need to do is look at the books that you are going to read and the people that you are going to associate with. To exemplify this notion, let's take a look at your children. How fearful do you get when they start reading the wrong books and more so, when associating with the wrong types of people? What makes your situation any different? If we are going to insist that our children are a product of their environment then why would we not recognize that we too are a product of our environment?

Henry Ford, inventor of the assembly line; Thomas Edison, inventor of the light bulb; Harvey Firestone, inventor of the modern day tractor tire; Charles Lindbergh, first person to cross the Atlantic by air; and Alexis Carrel, pioneer of organ transplant surgery: what do they all have in common? They are all titans in their industry. They were called the 'Five Uncommon Friends.' You see, every single one of them owned a summer home within the vicinity of each other and they would meet there a couple times a year. They played together, they ate together, they learned from each other and the number one question that they asked each other every time they met was "what new things have you learned since the last time we saw each other?"(10)

When we encounter the titans of our industries, do we run

away from them or do we try to learn from them? There is always something you can learn from your competition. There is no reason to have to fight with your competition. You can build businesses together.

Not so long ago I developed an interest in a specific real estate market. Calum DeSouza a successful developer from Belleview Properties, was more than willing to help me learn and grow. He realized the level of commitment I had towards this market.

I make this point because some may shy away from, or feel that they cannot approach, certain titans. They are passing up the chance to learn and grow from the best. Trust me when I say that these titans are well aware of the fact that they are only where they are in life, due to the aid and support that they received from others.

If they can truly acknowledge that your commitment is there, most of them will also be more then willing to help you along the way.

We are a product of the environment we create for ourselves. Some elements of that environment may be beyond our control, but we can control the development of our character. We are a collection of the books we read; the friends we keep; the activities we choose; the role models we emulate. What is your output now? What would you like it to be?

Garbage in equals garbage out. What you invest in yourself is what you will get out of yourself. There is no single, magical formula for creating success, mainly because success means something different to each and every one of us. There are unwavering principles that we can follow to insure our success. With a simple commitment to investing in yourself, you will find that you are well on your way to finding the solution. After the five years has passed, promise yourself that you will take a look back and reflect on how, in such a short period of time, your life could have changed so significantly. Was reading this book the catalyst? Likely not. Was it all the money spent on seminars and workshops? Again, I would highly doubt it. The truth of the matter is, the success you are destined to attain in the next five years will be a direct result of your commitment to that goal. The sooner you can divert your eyes from where you are, and focus them on where you are going, the sooner you will begin your ascent.

*"We are what we are today because of the books we've read and the people we have associated with for the last five years."*

# NOTES:
List 10 things you are willing to commit to doing
in order to invest in yourself.

# What Is Your Legacy?
## Conclusion

*"Leave behind a legacy of compassion"*

In your industry right now there is an individual with idealistic goals. This individual might very well be you. This person is intelligent, spry, quick-witted and tenacious. Survival is the first thing on their mind. Each morning they wake up knowing that they must outperform the largest of their competitors, or fall victim to them.

Also in your industry right now there is an established enterprise. This enterprise might very well be yours. This enterprise has unimaginable resources and seemingly wealth to match. It is trusted, respected, and solid, yet still innovative. 'Dominance' is in its mission statement. At the beginning of each business day this enterprise knows that it must remain as flexible as the smallest of their competitors or slowly lose market share and eventually starve.

Like the proverbial 'Gazelle and the Lion,' the gazelle

wakes up every morning knowing it has to run faster than the fastest lion or it will be eaten. A lion wakes up every morning knowing it has to run faster than the slowest gazelle or it will starve to death. The moral of the story? When the sun comes up, you had better be running.

As promised, I have had a lot of fun. I hope everybody takes away one thing with them -please keep in mind that we are surrounded by our circumstances. Everything is based, not what circumstances we have, but on the choices we make, based on those circumstances and the daily commitments that we make in our lives.

Desire is the starting point of all success. This fire needs to be lit from within. Everyone has it in them, they just have to be willing to go in and ignite it.

We should never settle for what is not in our hearts. At one point or another, in our lives, we have all had passion. If you are not happy with what you are doing, find your passion again, and follow the path that it leads you down.

The 7 Principles of Great Leaders will equip you with the means to excel, both in your industry, as well as in your personal life. They will inspire you and motivate you by getting you back in touch with your desire, passion, and purpose. Regardless of who we are or what we do, we all take on leadership roles. We must learn how to effectively lead ourselves before we can begin to effectively lead others.

In a world of constant change, these principles have stood unwavering throughout the course of time. By applying these principles to every aspect of your life, you will be able to effectively lead others through example.

I stopped dreaming because I got scared. I knew if I kept on dreaming I would become motivated, but I was not sure if I would follow through. I was scared of failing so I did not even try; I let go of my dreams and in turn failed with disgrace and regret. Until you get it in your heart you cannot get it in your head. We never have time enough for anything until we know why.

What are you going to leave behind on this planet once your physical life is over? Are you living for something that is greater than yourself? Greatness comes from beginning something that does not end with you. Enlightenment is only a thought away.

*"We Should Never Settle For What*
*Is Not In Our Hearts."*

# NOTES:

What are the 10 key points you have taken away from this book?

# NOTES:

List 20 things you want to learn or accomplish in your lifetime.

# NOTES:
What actions will you implement starting today?

References

1. "Abraham Lincoln Failures and Successes." <http://showcase.ne-tins.net/web/creative/lincoln/education/failures.htm>.

2. *www.angelfire.com*. Angel Fire. <http://www.angelfire.com/band/rickallenthundergod/bio.html>.

3. Armstrong, Lance. *It's Not About The Bike*. New York: Berkley, 2000.

4. "Building Big." *ww.pbs.org*. Public Broadcasting System. <http://www.pbs.org/wgbh/buildingbig/wonder/structure/brooklyn.html>.

5. Canfield, Jack. *The Success Principles*. New York: HarperCollins, 2005.

6. Carter-Scott, Cherie. *If Success is a Game These Are the Rules*. New York: Broadway, 2000.

7. Conner, James E., A 3rd Serving of Chicken Soup for the Soul (Mary Groda)

8. Covey, Stephen . *The 7 Habits of Highly Effective People*. New York: Free Press, 1989.

9. "www.dreamjobcoaching.com." Dream Job Coaching. <http://zines.webvalence.com/sites/DreamJob/Broadcast.D19990401.html>. (disney / ford)

10. Five Uncommon Friends Foundation. <http://www.uncommon-friends.org/>.

11. "Franchising Home." McDonalds. <http://www.mcdonalds.com/content/corp/franchise/franchisinghome.html>.

12. Hansen, Mark Victor. *The One Minute Millionaire*. New York: Harmony Books, 2002 (Rocky Story).

13. Peters, Thomas. *In Search of Excellence*. New York: Warner Books, 1982.

14. "www.puredueexponent.com." The Exponent. <http://www.purdueexponent.org/2001/09/04/opinions/>.

15. Sharma, Robin. "www.robinsharma.com." *Robin Sharma—Leadership, Proffesional Speaker*. <http://www.robinsharma.com/articles1.html>. (Children)

16. Sharma, Robin. *The Monk Who Sold His Ferrari*. Toronto: Harper Collins, 1997.

17. Tzu, Sun. *The Art of War*. : , .

18. Robbins, Anthony. *Unlimited Power*. : , .

19. "A Womans Place." Storty Bin. <http://www.storybin.com/builders/builders160.shtml>.

20. Lowitt, Bruce. "Banister stuns the world with 4-minute mile." *St. Petersburg Times* 17 December 1999: .

21. Bennet-Goleman, Tara. Emotional Alchemy. New York: Three Rivers Press, 2001

## ABOUT THE AUTHOR

Fred Sarkari coaches, teaches and provides management consulting services to a broad range of organizations from start ups to some of the World's largest organizations. As a presenter, Fred's unique approach combines vision with practical application, delivering a customized and personally tailored message with warmth and humour to each audience member. This approach provides a compelling and practical message to audiences regardless of size and translates through to the programs he creates.

## KEYNOTES AND SEMINARS WITH
## FRED SARKARI

Fred Sarkari: Leadership for Life ™ is a unique sales and personal development company, that seeks to empower individuals and organizations to achieve their visions, goals and dreams.

Fred Sarkari believes that people are a company's greatest asset. Leadership for Life workshops and seminars give your organization the opportunity to expose your team to a wealth of practical knowledge and hands-on activities through personal and case study analysis. We are passionate about our Leadership for Life programs because we have seen them work time and time again!

Our focus is the development of the individual. We believe that people are the foundation of any organization, with each person impacting the dynamic of the whole body. The success of your organization is the by-product of individual successes.

Fred has facilitated numerous workshops for employees of various companies including: Coca-Cola · Home Depot · CIBC · Microsoft · Royal Bank · North West Mutual Funds · Ceridian · Scotia Bank · Fuji · ReMax · Promotional Products Association · BMO Bank of Montreal · Genworth Financial (formerly GE Mortgage) · Royal Le Page · FirstLine Mortgages · Midas · Four Seasons Hotels · Wellsfargo and many more.

Fred Sarkari provides services to organizations internationally. To book Fred for your next conference or workshop please visit www.fredsarkari.com or contact fred@fredsarkari.com / 800.742.2379

## PERSONAL COACHING
## WITH FRED SARKARI

The benefits of coaching are truly endless, as a coach helps you to achieve your personal desired state. The most impactful benefits are linked to our coaching process for it is customized to each individual and focuses on their specific needs. Most times we our selves are not aware of what it is that we truly need, nor are we always aware of our present situation.

Through our assessment system we will help you to become aware of your specific needs and create a strategy that would benefit you.

Clients can have a variety of outcomes in mind when they get a coach: Such as, career and business, personal relationship, or finding personal direction, passion and purpose. They may want to double their income, get the most out of business pursuits, or simply have more joy in life.

Fred Sarkari will help you:

•Increase self awareness

•Unlock your potential and talents

•Discover more of your authentic self

•Achieve the life you truly want

Coaching with Fred Sarkari is completely customized for your personal needs.

Please contact coaching@fredsarkari.com / 800.742.2379 for more information.

# I WOULD LOVE TO HEAR FROM YOU

I would like to thank every individual who has in their own humble and compassionate way taken the time to help me in my journey to this day. To this I am very grateful and fortunate.

If you have had the experience to sit into one of my conferences, workshops or read this book, I hope it was evident how much I love what I do and the passion that I have for it.

My greatest reward is when I know that my work has made an impact in one's life. It would be my honor if you would take the time to share some of your success stories on how this book or any of our conferences has affected your personal or professional life.

I thank you all for giving my life purpose!

## COMPANY CULTURE

To order copies of this book for your company, please contact customerservice@fredsarkari.com for a bulk discount.

# INSPIRE OUR YOUTH

## Mission Statement
*Building hope for the future,*
*in the hearts & minds of our youth.*

Inspire Our Youth foundation was created by Fred Sarkari-Leadership for Life. We believe that every individual has what it takes to achieve the life that they know they are destined to live; therefore our purpose is to create awareness of inspiration that already exists within our youth. By instilling; desire, direction, passion and most importantly purpose, they may continue to create their own belief system enabling them to lead a full and productive life.

In order to create a value based family life Inspire Our Youth not only works with our youth, but with their parents as well. As parents we need to set the example of what defines leadership so our children can be tomorrow's leaders. Today's youth need to develop a way of thinking that will instill life-long values they will need in order to prosper, to fight for what is right, to fight for what they believe, to become the person they know within themselves to be no matter the obstacles they are facing.

## SUPPORT FROM THE COMMUNITY
Inspire Our Youth is run on support from the community by forging relationships with other organizations. Any support you or your organization can provide in conjunction with Inspire Our Youth is appreciated, if you can help in any way please contact us.